BARNES-BAILEY GENEALOGY

BARNES-BAILEY
GENEALOGY

COMPILED BY WALTER D. BARNES

1939

WALTER D. BARNES
3603 CALLAWAY AVENUE
BALTIMORE, MARYLAND

Notice

In many older books, foxing (or discoloration) occurs and, in some instances, print lightens with wear and age. Reprinted books, such as this, often duplicate these flaws, notwithstanding efforts to reduce or eliminate them. The pages of this reprint have been digitally enhanced and, where possible, the flaws eliminated in order to provide clarity of content and a pleasant reading experience.

Barnes-Bailey Genealogy

Originally published:
Baltimore, 1939

Reprinted by

Janaway Publishing, Inc.
732 Kelsey Ct.
Santa Maria, California 93454
(805) 925-1038
www.janawaygenealogy.com

2015

ISBN: 978-1-59641-364-1

FOREWORD

The information contained in this genealogy was obtained by consulting old family Bibles, inscriptions on tomb stones, records of the Maryland Historical Society (Baltimore), The Hall of Records (Annapolis), and through the splendid co-operation of many of the family with personal contributions.

In order to enable the reader to trace his ancestry in this record each generation is compiled separately, and is represented by a letter; thus A, the first generation, B the second and so on.

The name at the top of the page designates the Family; the letter and number in parenthesis ( ) directly under 'Issue of - - -' refers to the father's or mother's record in the preceding generation; the letter and number in parenthesis ( ) following the name of the Child refers to the Issue of its marriage in the following generation.

The Letter and Number after the name in the Index refers to the Generation and Page Number found in the upper right hand corner of each page.

b.=born; m.=married; d.=died or dead.

WALTER D. BARNES (I-17),
3603 Callaway Ave.,
Baltimore, Maryland.

November, 1939.

BURIAL LOCATIONS

(*) Bay View Cemetery, better known as "Coen's Hill." On Chapel Road, three miles from Havre de Grace, Md.

(**) Wesleyan Chapel Cemetery.

(†) Harmony (Presbyterian) Church Cemetery.

(‡) Rock Run (Methodist) Church Cemetery.
            (*All near Havre de Grace, Md.*)

(§) Angel Hill Cemetery, at Havre de Grace, Md.

(¶) Churchville (Presbyterian) Church Cemetery, at Churchville, Md.

BARNES

The name of *Barnes* is said by some authorities to have been taken from the Norse word *bjorne*, meaning 'warrior', probably being given to its bearer for prowess on the field of battle.

Early trace of the *Barnes* race is found in the Southeastern part of England, and indicate Dano-Norman Origin, probably coming to England at the time England was under Norman Kings, 1000-1154, although one of the name appears to have been a general in the service of William the Conqueror when he entered England in 1066.

The DOMESDAY BOOK, or DOOMSDAY BOOK, is a statistical account of the state of England in the latter part of the eleventh century, prepared by command of William the Conqueror, in the year or years just preceding 1086. It contains a record of what property every inhabitant of England possessed in land or in cattle, and how much money this was worth. It is one of the oldest and most valuable of English Historical Records.

In this Book will be found the name of EARL BERNE (pronounced Barn), descended from the Royal House of Denmark.

'The Berne' is described as 'an urban district of Surrey, in the parliamentary burrough of Richmond', and has in its Church of St. Mary's, an armoured effigy of William Millebourne, dating from 1460.

'The Berne' was visited by Queen Elizabeth and was later the home of the poet Cowley.

One of the earlier branches of the family in England was that represented in County Essex about the beginning of the thirteenth century by Sir Giles (whom another authority calls 'William') Barneis or Barnes, who was the father of Sir Randall or Sir Ralph, who had a son named Sir Ralph, who was the father of Sir Edward or Edmond, who was the father of Sir John, who was the father of Sir James, Richard, Sir Thomas (to be mentioned later), and William; of whom Sir James was the father of Sir Richard, who became Lord Barnes and was the father by his wife, Phillipe Dalyngridge, of a daughter named Margaret.

Sir Thomas Barnes of County Essex, before mentioned, son of Sir John, married Catherine Stoner and was the father by her of Sir James and Thomas, of whom the latter settled in County Surrey, and was the father by his wife Margaret St. Jermyn, of John, who was the father of a son named John, who left issue of two sons, John and William, of whom the latter resided in County Essex, and was the father by his wife Dorothy Hansard of William, Thomas, Leonard, Richard, and several daughters. Their son William was the father of a son named Thomas, while his brother Leonard was the father of a son named Anthony.

About the year 1400 a Robert Barnes was living in Worcestershire, England. He was the grand-father of John Barnes, who married a Miss Wilkinton and was the father by her of William, who had issue by his wife Alice Midelmore, of William, Richard, Edward, Thomas and several daughters.

In the latter part of the fifteenth century John Barnes of Dorsetshire was the father of Robert and John, of whom the first married Elizabeth Hodder, and was the father by her of Robert, John and Thomas, of whom the last married Bridget Mill and was the father by her of a son named Henry, who had issue by his wife Bridget Lambert of Thomas and Anne.

In the early part of the sixteenth century Bartholomew Barnes was living in London, although he appears to have owned estates in Essex. He was the father of, among others, a son named Thomas, who was the father by his wife Anne Brookesby of Thomas and Bartholomew and Anne, of whom the first had issue by his first wife Anne, of Richard, Bartholomew and several daughters, as well as by his second wife, Isabelle Harvey, of James and others.

Among the other early records of England are those of Henry de la Berne of County Norfolk, Richard de la Berne of County Kemp, William de la Berne of Dorsetshire, John and Henry atte Berne of Somersetshire, William de la Barne of Yorkshire, and Walter de la Barne of Lincolnshire about the year 1273; those of Richard le Barne and Thomas le Barne of Yorkshire before 1370; those of Mayor John Barnes of London in 1370; those of Reverend Robert Barnes, chaplain to King Henry the Eighth; and those of Reverend Richard Barnes, Bishop of Nottingham in 1567, whose son Barnaby was Lord Mayor of London for many years.

While it is not definitely known in every case from which of the many illustrious lines of the family in England the first emigrants of the name to America were descended, it is generally believed that all of the Barnes families were of extremely ancient and honorable lineage.

One of the first by the name to come to America was John Barnes, who settled at Plymouth, Mass., before 1632 and married Mary Plummer by whom he had issue of Esther, John, Jonathan, Lydia, Hannah and Mary.

As early as 1637 Thomas Barnes came from County Norfolk, England, and settled at Hingham, Mass. By his wife Ann he was the father of Thomas, John, Elizabeth, Ann, Hannah or Sarah, James and Peter.

Another Thomas Barnes settled at Hartford, Conn., before 1639 and later removed to Farmington, in the same colony. He left issue there by his wife Mary Andrus or Andrews, of Thomas and Ebenezer, as well as (possibly by a former wife) of Sarah, Benjamin and Joseph.

Richard Barnes the son of Richard and Agnes Barnes of Hampshire, England, came to Marlborough, Mass., with his widowed mother about 1639. By his wife, Deborah Dix, whom he married in 1667, he was the father of Sarah, Richard, Deborah, John, Edward and Abigail.

Sometime before 1640 William Barnes came from County Norfolk, England, to Salisbury, Mass. By his wife, Rachel, he was the father of Mary, William, Hannah, Deborah, Jonathan, Rachel, Sarah and Rebecca.

Matthew Barnes, who was living at Braintree and Boston, Mass., about 1640, was the father by his wife Rebecca, of Alice and Hannah, and by his second wife, the Widow Elizabeth Hunt, of a daughter named Sarah and a son John.

Another Thomas Barnes settled at New Haven, Conn., with his brother Daniel, of whom however, nothing further is known, sometime before 1643. By his wife Elizabeth, this Thomas was the father of John, Elizabeth, Thomas, Mercy, Abigail, Daniel, Martha and Maybee (a son).

Another Thomas Barnes came from London to America in 1658 and settled at Marlborough, Mass. He was the father of at least one son, named Thomas.

There was also a Thomas Barnes living at Swanzey, Mass., before 1669, who left by his first wife Prudence the following children, Lydia, Thomas, Sarah, Elizabeth, Anne, John, Peter, Samuel and Hannah.

Among the numerous others of the name who came to America in the seventeenth century were Edward of Elizabeth City County, Va., in 1623; Joshua of Yarmouth, Mass., in 1632; Lancelot of Elizabeth City County, Va., in 1632; Barnaby of Charles City County, and James of James City County, Va., in 1637; Edward of Accomac County and Henry of Isle of Wight County, Va., in 1639; Obadiah, of New Haven, Conn., in 1640; and William of the Isle of Wight County, Va., before 1642; Martin of Virginia in 1642; Henry, George, William, Stephen, Charles and John of Northumberland County, Va., about 1650; John of Concord, Mass., before 1661; Charles of Easthampton, L. I., in 1663.

There were also 35 by this name that settled in Maryland between 1655 and 1676, nine of whom were women, the names of the men follow: Anthony in 1663; Charles in 1668; Christopher in 1666; Clement in 1664; Daniel in 1671; Francis in 1666; Francis in 1667; Francis, Jr. in 1666; James, 1663; James in 1676; John in 1659; John in 1662; John in 1662; John in

1663; John in 1664; John in 1666; John in 1670; John in 1675; Joshua in 1672; Richard in 1672; Samuel in 1664; Steven in 1671; Thomas in 1666; Thomas in 1674; Walter in 1655 and WILLIAM who sailed from Hull, England and landed in 1669, the one who was the fore-father of the Genealogy which is to follow.

(Refer to A-1)

BAILEY

The name of BAILEY or BAYLEY was probably derived from the French *Baille* and originally meant "castle or fortified city." *Bailie*, however, was also a Scottish term, meaning "a superior officer or magistrate." The name is found on ancient records in the spelling of Bayly, Bayley, Bailleu, Bailey, and Bailleul, of which Bailleu and Bailleul were the ancient French forms.

Some family historians assert that the family is descended from John Baliol, King of Scotland at an extremely early date. There seems to be more conclusive evidence, however, that most of the name are of ancient French descent. There may have been, in very remote times, two entirely separate families of the name, one French and the other Scottish.

There was a family of Bailleuls, Chatelains of Bailleul, in that part of France known as Normandy as early as 1052 A. D. At that time Simon, son of Arnoul de Gramines, was the representative of the Bailleuls. His sons or grandsons, Albert and Baudouin de Bailleul, are on the list of Flemish knights who took active part in the First Crusade to the Holy Land.

Baudouin, son of Baudouin, married Euphemie de Saint-Omer and had two sons, Gerard and Hoston, and two daughters, Alix and Mathilde. There is reason to believe that he had other children, among whom were Hector and Oston.

Some of the members of this family held the titles of Lords of Doulieu and Eecke, and others went into England in the early fifteenth century. One branch of the English family settled at Willow Hall in the person of Jacques de Bailleu at the beginning of the seventeenth century.

Another English line was that of Thomas Bayly who married in 1567 in the parish of Bromham, Wiltshire. By his first wife Anne he was the father of Daniel, Joel, Thomas, and Rebecca; and by his second wife Jane he had further issue of two children, of whom the first died young and the second was named John.

Daniel, eldest son of Thomas, removed to Westbrook, parish of Bromham, and was the progenitor of one of the New England lines of the family. He was the father by his wife Mary of Thomas, Daniel, Mary, Dorothy, Ann, Josias, Joel, and Isaac.

Of some prominence in Great Britain, where the Baileys and Bayleys were in many cases of the landed gentry and yeomanry, the family was well represented among the earliest British colonists in the New World.

One of the first of the family to emigrate to America was John Bailey who settled at Salisbury, Mass., in 1635. He was from Chippenham, Wiltshire. He left a son Robert and two daughters in England and brought with him another son John and a daughter Johanna. Johanna married William Huntington in 1640.

John, son of the immigrant John, married Eleanor Emery and made his home at Newbury. Their children were Rebecca, John, Sarah, Joshua, Joseph, James, Isaac, Rachel, Judith, and two others who died young.

According to some accounts Henry Bayley of Salisbury may have been another son of the immigrant John. He had issue by his wife Rebecca of two children, Henry and Rebecca.

In the year 1638 Richard Bailey came from Southampton to Lyon, Mass. He married Edna Lambert and had a son named Joseph.

Joseph, son of Richard, removed to Salem. He had issue by his wife Abigail of Abigail, Richard, and perhaps others.

Thomas Bayley was residing in Weymouth, Mass., prior to the year 1640 and may have been previously of Virginia. He was the father of John, Thomas, Samuel, and Esther.

John, son of Thomas, had two children by his wife Hannah. They were John and Thomas.

Thomas, son of the immigrant Thomas, married Ruth Porter in the year 1660. He was the father by her of Christian, Samuel, Mary, Sarah, Ruth, Martha, and Thomas.

Samuel, youngest son of the immigrant Thomas, had issue by his wife Mary of Samuel, Mary, James, John, and Joseph.

In the year 1640 James Bailey came to Salem, Mass., from England. He was the brother of Richard of Lynn and the father of John, Lydia, Jonathan, Damaris, James, Thomas, and Samuel. Of these, Jonathan died young, and Samuel and Thomas died without issue.

John, eldest son of the immigrant James, married Mary Mighill in 1668. They were the parents of Jonathan, Ann, Nathaniel, Thomas, James, Mary, Elizabeth, Lydia, and John.

James, son of the immigrant James, married Elizabeth Johnson in 1680. He made his home at Rowley, Mass., and was the father of James, Elizabeth, John, Hannah, James, and Samuel.

Guido Bayley made his home at Salem sometime before the year 1642. He was the father by his wife Elizabeth of two children, Elizabeth and Joseph.

Another early immigrant was Jonas Bayley who came to Scarborough in 1650. He married, first, Elizabeth Dearing, and second, Elinor Jackson, both widows. Little is known of him or his family.

In 1652 Thomas Bayley was living at New London, Conn. Two years later he married Lydia Redfield, by whom he had issue of Mary, Thomas, John, William, James, Joseph, and Lydia.

A few years later a William Bailey became a resident of Newport, R. I. He married Grace Parsons and had John, Joseph, Edward, Hugh, and Stephen.

In 1661 Samuel Bailie of Weymouth had his first child Mary by his wife of the same name. His other children were James, John, and Joseph.

John Bailey, an early settler at Scituate, Mass., married Sarah White in 1673. Their offspring were John, Sarah, Mary, Joseph, Benjamin, William, Hannah, and Samuel.

Joel Bayley, of the Westbrook line of the family, came with his brother Daniel to Chester County, Pa., about the year 1681. They were the owners of much land and the holders of many public offices. Joel married Ann Short and had issue by her of Mary, Ann, Daniel, Isaac, Joel, Thomas, John, and Josiah. The descendants of Daniel are not of record.

Two brothers, the Reverend John and the Reverend Thomas, came to New England about the year 1683 and settled at Watertown. The Reverend John married twice, first, Lydia, and second, Susanna, but died without issue. The Reverend Thomas had issue by his wife Rebecca of two sons, John and Thomas.

More recent representatives of these various branches of the Bailey or Bayley families have spread to every State of the Union and have made a worthy contribution to the rise of the American nation. Outstanding traits of the family as a whole include courage, fortitude, industry, strength of will, and strong faith in God and in humanity. Members of the family have been particularly outstanding in the fields of science, law, religion, mathematics, and education.

Among those of the name who fought as officers in the Revolutionary War were Colonel John Bailey, of Massachusetts; Brigadier General Jacob Bailey or Bayley, of Vermont; Captain John Bailey, of Virginia; Captain Lemuel Bailey, of Rhode Island; and Captain Joshua Bayley, of New Hampshire.

John, Joseph, Joshua, Thomas, Samuel, Henry, and Richard are some of the Christian names most favored by the family for its male progeny.

From the 'List of Early Settlers' at the Maryland Historical Society we find the following with the dates of their arrival in Maryland:

Andrew, 1651; Charles, 1673; Elizabeth, 1677; GEORGE, 1677; Godfrey, 1663; John, 1673; Mary, 1663; Robert, 1653; Robert, 1654; Robert, 1674; Stephen, 1674; Thomas, 1658, and Thomas BAILEY, 1678.

Also came Elizabeth, 1658; Elizabeth, 1663; Elizabeth, 1673; Elizabeth, 1676; Francis, 1676; John, 1658; John, 1661; John, 1666; Phillip, 1649; Richard, 1658; Richard, 1674; Thomas, 1674; Tobias, 1656; and William BAYLEY in 1674.

In 1673 came Thomas BAYLIE.

Ambrose in 1668; George, 1671; George, 1674; Godfrey, 1659; James, 1674; James, 1676; John, 1663; John, 1667; John, 1669; Mary, 1663; Nicholas, 1673; Richard, 1658; Sarah, 1674 and William BAYLY in 1676,

(Refer to A-2)

Born 1655 ?;   Married 1675 ?;   Died May 22, 1720.

It has been a tradition in the family that William was our first ancestor in this Country, and the writer has in his possession three separate epistles, each coming from a family of one of the grandsons of this man, purporting to set forth this fact; the first coming through the family of FORD and was given me by the family of the late Edwin Barnes (G-8) of Philadelphia, which sets forth the name of William as the first of this genealogy; the second, through JOB is from the pen of the late Albert P. Silver, of Harford Co. (Md.), who states that he consulted one of the family who was very much interested in the record and was "assured beyond a doubt" that William was our forefather; the third, through JAMES, was written by the late Septimus Davis, also of Harford Co., who says that he has considerable data regarding the Barnes Family and is endeavoring to find out "when William came over."

The writer located the information regarding the arrival of William and a copy from the LAND RECORDS, Annapolis, Md., follows:

"Liber 13, folio 1.

"A list of servants names brought into Maryland by the Nightengale, ketch of Hull, (Eng.) John Hobson, Master, A. D. 1669

IMPRIMIS
Thomas Daniell   Abell Hill
Daniell Seapington   Joseph Winters
Robert Gott   Catherine Thomsone
Thomas Story   John Perkinson
Valentine Barton   John Inchboard
Thomas Clarke   Thomas Tindall
Henry Watson   Richard Brogden
Anthony Watson   Elizabeth Beaford
John Hunter   Ellinor Gernty
Richard Brogden   Thomas Hemvicke
Charles Abell   John Stronge
William White   WILLIAM BARNE"

"September 21st, 1670

"Came Thomas Wilborne of the County of Anne Arundel, Merchant, and proved right to One Thousand Two Hundred acres of land to him due for transportation of the several persons above named and desired warrant for the same.

"Warrant then issued to lay out for the said Thomas Wilborne, One Thousand Two Hundred acres of land being due him for transporting the several persons aforesaid."

William was born in England, and as no one has made an effort to learn the date of his birth, it is unknown, however, inasmuch as he lived in this Country 51 years after his arrival in 1669, leads us to believe that he was very young when transported. His name being the last on the passenger list also lends strength in this respect. Hence, let us assume that he was born around 1655. In consideration of the family that followed we can also assume that he was married about 1675, although no record of the marriage has been located.

William evidently spent most of his life in the neighborhood of Herring Creek, Anne Arundel County, which is located about eighteen miles below Annapolis and near Tracy's Landing, for it was here that his son Job met and married Elizabeth Ford (see Deed of July 8, 1706, B-1a).

Thomas Ford, the father of Elizabeth, in 1670 purchased from Henry Stockett 300 acres of land called "Repulta" (see Deed July 8, 1706, B-1a). This land was situated in the upper part of what is now Havre de Grace, and through Will, half of this parcel went to Thomas Ford's daughter, Elizabeth Barnes.

Job having died suddenly while a young man, we assume that Elizabeth and her children, with her father-in-law, William, moved over to "Repulta" as we are able to locate the death of William as May 22, 1720, recorded at St. George's Parrish, also known as Spesutie Church, located near Perryman, Harford Co., Md. This (Episcopal) Church is located about 9 or 10 miles from "Repulta" and entirely too far for such record had they still been living in Anne Arundel County.

We do not know how many children William left, but we do know that our genealogy continues with

JOB (B-1)

Transported 1677 Thomas Applewaite, of

London, (Eng.) Commander of the 'Crown Milligo.'

Apl. 3, 1677 Came John Warner and proved his right to fourteen hundred and fifty acres of land for transporting,

Richard Cooper	John Davys
Abraham Rowse	Richard Cordywn
Mary Long	Robert Willson
Edward Paine	Edward Hunt
Anthony Young	Thomas Gold
William Oram	Richard Osborn
Arthur Bradley	Elizabeth Beckford
William Custan	Bridgett Hubbard
GEORGE BAILY	Ann Hinxman
William Glover	Elizabeth Nedham
Robert West	Thomas Ford
John Gage	Isaac Price
Benjamin Gray	John Hughes
Thomas Mason	Edw. Wheeler

and John Roach
into the Province to inhabitate.

I Thomas Warner do hereby assign over unto Edward Parrish twenty-nine rights to land to have and to hold the same, unto him the said Edward to his heirs and assigns forever.

Witness my hand and seal Apl. 3d, 1677.

Test; Nic Painter

Thomas Warner   (Sealed)

(LAND RECORDS, Annapolis, Md., Liber 15, pp. 452.)

(There is no absolute certainty that this person was the father of George Bailey (B-2) and the only assumption is that of namesake; we do know, however, that all those who follow George Bailey (B-2) are his descendants.)

(See Second Generation B-2.)

Born, 1676?;   Married, 1697?;   Died, 1703.

'To all X^tian People Wee Matthias Clark of Herring Creek in Anne Arundel County in the Province of Maryland, Carpenter and Elizabeth the wife of the s/d Matthias, the widdow of Job Barnes of the place and County aforesaid, Planter, Deceased, the only daughter of Thomas Ford, of the same place, Deceased—'.

From the above paragraph taken from deed of July 8, 1706 which follows we learn that Job married
ELIZABETH FORD
being the only daughter of Thomas Ford and that they lived in Herring Creek, and that Job was a Planter. No record as to date of marriage has been located.

Job, husband of Elizabeth died in the fall of 1703, without having left a Will, for we find recorded in Testamentary Proceedings, Liber 20, folio 39 the following;

'Oct. 11, 1703

WHEREAS it has pleased God to take away my beloved husband Job Barnes, it is my desire that William Smith Administer upon my husbands estate.

(her)
Elizabeth X Barnes.'
(mark)

After the death of her husband Elizabeth married Matthias Clark and gave birth to a daughter, Elizabeth, born July 22, 1705 and died Dec. 5th 1706.

Elizabeth married her third husband, John Norton (see Deed of Oct. 23, 1735 which follows) and by him gave birth to five children, William, John & Richard, Mary, Ann Elizabeth.
John Norton died in 1727.

Elizabeth outlived all of her husbands and although we have been unable to locate any record of the date of her death we assume that she died in Baltimore (now Harford) County, as Deed of Oct. 23, 1735 where she gives her holdings in 'Repulta' to her loving son, Ford Barnes, she mentions as being 'of Baltimore County'.

As previously stated, we therefore assume that Elizabeth with her children, all of whom were young and her father-in-law, William Barnes, took up their residence on 'Repulta' for we also find the Baptisms at St. George's Parrish of her children by Job Barnes. This record being made after December 1713.

Job and Elizabeth had three children, all boys;

FORD

JOB

JAMES

(see Third Generation)
(C-1)

Thomas Ford, father of Elizabeth, Transported June 1652. ABH 348.

DEED MADE July 8, 1706.

To all X^tian People Wee Matthias Clark of Herring Creek in Anne Arundel County in the Province of Maryland, Carpenter and Elizabeth the wife of the s/d Matthias, the widdow of Job Barnes of the place and County aforesaid, Planter, Deceased, the only daughter of Thomas Ford of the same place, Deceased, send greetings;

WHEREAS—Cecilius the Lord Proprietor of the Providence aforesaid by his deed of grant under ye great seal dated ye four and twentieth day of September in the year of our Lord God 1663 Did grant unto Henry Stockett, Gent a certain tract or parcel of land called Repulta containing three hundred acres more or less lying on the west side of the Chesapeake Bay on the west side of a river in the said Bay called Susquehanna River in ye County of Baltimore in the Province aforesaid Beginning at a marked Locust Tree standing on a small point by the river side respecting the lower end of Palmer Island to the East, running for breadth north & by west up the river one hundred and fifty perches to a marked Chestnut Oake bounding on the north by a line drawn west from the the oake for the length of three hundred and twenty perches, on the west side by a line drawn southeast from the end of the west line for breadth one hundred and fifty perches, on the south by a line drawn east from the end of the south & by east Line unto the marked Locust on the east by the a/fd River, containing three hundred acres, more or less, and WHEREAS the said Henry Stockett did by indenture under his hand seal dated thirteenth day of December in the year of our Lord God 1670 convey and make over all his right, title and interest of the tract or parcel of land unto Thomas Ford of Herring Creek a/fd & to his heirs forever and whereas James Ford, son and heir of Thomas Ford aforesaid named by his last will and testament dated the eighth and twentieth day of July in the year of our Lord God 1702 Did thereby give, devise and bequeath unto his loving brother John Ford and his loving sister Elizabeth Barnes all that tract or parcel of land called the Repulta containing three hundred acres, more or less, lying on the Susquehanna River in Baltimore County a/fd to be equally divided them and their heirs and assigns forever as by the a/fd will more fully and at large appeareth AND WHEREAS also the s/d Matthias Clark hath been cast into prison by a Law Suite contracted from a certain debt by the s/d Elizabeth when she was ye widdow of Job Barnes in order for the sale of her part of ye a/fd tract whereby the s/d Matthias Clark hath been forced to sell and part with a certain tract of land in Herring Creek a/fd lately purchased of Thomas Tonch, Esq. for his two sons John Clark and Webber Clark, Therefore know ye that we the said Matthias Clark and Elizabeth the wife of the s/d Matthias for the consideration above set forth & for Divers other good causes and considerations HAVE given, granted and assigned and by this our present Deed of Gift do give, grant, assign, assure and make over unto John Clark and Webber Clark, sons of the said Matthias Clark and to their and each of their heirs or assigns, two full third parts of the Moiety or half, or half parts of the aforesaid tract or parcel of land whether divided or undivided as both belong to us, the said Matthias Clark and Elizabeth my wife by virtue of the last will and testament of her brother James Ford before named and known by the name of Repulta lying on the west of the Susquehanna River in Baltimore County a/fd containing three hundred acres of land according to ye marks & bounds first sett forth & prescribed, TO HAVE AND TO HOLD the s/d two third parts of ye said Moiety or half parts of ye a/fd tract or parcel of land whether divided or undivided hereby given, granted and assigned & every part and parcel thereof together with full ingress, egress, regress and other full Privileges and benefits thereunto belonging unto the s/d John Clark and Webber Clark, their and each of their heirs, assigns forever and wee the said Matthias Clark and Elizabeth the wife of the s/d Matthias Do further by those presents Grant, Assure and promise that wee the s/d Matthias Clark and Elizabeth the wife of the s/d Matthias, our heirs and assigns upon the reasonable request of the said John Clark and Webber Clark, their or either of their heirs or assigns shall and will make, acknowledge, suffer, Execute all & every further & other act or acts, thing or things, assurances and conveyances whatsoever as by the s/d John Clark and Webber Clark, their or either of their assigns, or their or either of their Counsel learned in the law shall from time to time reasonably Devised or advised for the further & better assurance, Surety and sure making of the Promises, that is to say of the said two full third parts of the Moiety or halfe parte of the aforesaid tract or parcel of land called Repulta containing three hundred acres of land, more or less, lying in Baltimore County a/fd unto ye s/d John Clark and Webber Clark, their or either of their heirs and assigns forever, according to the true intent and meaning of this present writing or Deed of Gift Beit by fine or recovery . . . Deed or Deeds Inrolled or not Inrolled and recording of those presents or by all, any or as many of the s/d means or ways or by any other Law, rule or reasonable testamonies whatsoever. In Witness whereof the said Matthais Clark and Elizabeth his wife have hereunto sett their hands and seales this eighth day of July in the year of our Lord God One Thousand Seven Hundred and Six.

his
MATTHIAS X CLARK
mark

her
ELIZABETH X CLARK,
mark

July 8, 1706

The writer is unable to explain why Elizabeth, after having deeded a part of Repulta to John and Webber Clark, as per above deed, later deeds all her portion to "my loving son, Ford Barnes", as described in deed which follows.

The records show that Webber Clark, conveyed by deed, his interest in Repulta to Ephriam Gover, May 27, 1732. Liber 1 S L pp. 249.

From Wills of Ford Barnes, C-1a; Ford Barnes, D-1a and Amos Barnes, E-1a, we find this tract or a part thereof being handed down from one generation to another.

M-323 DEED Elizabeth Norton to Ford Barnes.

To all CHRIST. PEOPLE to whom these presents shall come, I, Elizabeth Norton of Baltimore County and Province of Maryland send greetings,

KNOW YE that Elizabeth Norton for and in consideration of the love, good will and affection which I have and do hold toward my loving son, Ford Barnes of the County and Province aforesaid HAVE given and granted and by these presents do fully, freely, clearly and absolutely give and grant to the said Ford Barnes, his heirs and assigns all that one certain piece & parcel of land situated lying & being in aforesaid County and Province and on the west side of the Susquehanna River called and known by RUPUL-TER, beginning at a bounded Locust Tree standing on a small point respecting the lower end of Palmer Island running thence up the river north by west it intersects with Samuel Govers land then running with said land 320 perch, then running south 75 perch, then with a straight line to the first beginning Tree, estimated two hundred acres, more or less TOGETHER with all the right, title, interest, claim and demand whatsoever which I now have or which my or either of my heirs or assigns may hereafter have of to or in the said granted Possession or any part thereof TO HAVE AND TO HOLD the said tract of land and all and singular other the Possessions herein mentioned with the appurteances unto him the said Ford Barnes, his heirs and assigns forever absolutely without any incumbrance of condition as I the said Elizabeth Norton have fully, freely and absolutely and of my own accord set and put in further testimony. In witness hereof I have hereunto set my hand and seal this twenty-third day of October in the year of our Lord One Thousand Seven Hundred and Thirty-five.

her
ELIZABETH X NORTON
mark.

Oct. 23, 1735

LIBER M, pp 323.

Issue of GEORGE & ————— (?)
(A-2)

GEORGE   (C2) b.   d.   1754
                      m.   Sarah Maclane
                      b.   d.

(dau. of Hector Maclain (d. 1722) of
Balto. Co., and granddaughter of Hec-
tor Maclane of St. Mary's Co. and his
wife Sarah Morgan, dau. of Capt.
Thomas Morgan (d. 1697) of that
County.

The seal of George Bailey shows the crest of Northallerton, Yorkshire.
(Eng.)

(Md. Historical Magazine, Vol. 16; pp 194.)

GEORGE BAILEY and other neighbors of Josephus Murray petitioned the Court with reference the cleaning of a road located Indian Road (now Court Road) and Garrison Rd. Also road overseer as follows;

'It is evident that the Court intended to divide the rolling road which ran from Capt. Philip Jones' quarter on Soldiers Delight to the Iron Works Landing, between the overseers of Soldiers Delight Hundred and Patapsco Upper Hundred respectively.

Soldiers Delight was created Nov. 1733 and was divided from Patapsco Upper Hundred by the Old Indian or Court Road.—The Court appointed George Bailey overseer of the roads 'from the Soldiers Delight to the landing at then head of Patapsco, from John Belt, Jr., plantation in the forrest to the said landing'.

'In the same month of August 1728, the Court appointed—George Bailey overseer of the roads 'from the main falls by Christopher Randall's to Gwins Falls where the road, passes to the widow Hansons Mill, and from Bens Run by the plantation where Zebediah Baker now lives to the aforesaid place of Gwins Falls'.

(Balto Co. Court Proceedings, Liber I. W. S. No. 6, 1728-30, f. 26 et seq.)

Hansons Mill was situated on Jones Falls at Bath Street. The road between the Mill and Christopher Randall's plantation must have crossed Gwinns Falls either at the ford or a short distance above Mount Clare Mill or at the second fork at Brunswick Street Bridge.

I am inclined to think that the road which ran from Bens Run by the plantation where Zebediah Baker lived to the same ford of Gwinns Falls as that where the road to Christopher Randall's crossed, was the predecessor of the Old Frederick Road by Ellicotts Upper Mills.

(Md. Hist. Magazine. Vol. 16, pp 245.)

Will of GEORGE BAILEY. May 25, 1754

In the name of God, Amen, I George Bailey of Baltimore County in the Province of Maryland, Planter being weak in body but of sound mind and memory (Blessed be God) do this twenty-fifth day of May in the year seventeen hundred and fifty four, make and publish this my last Will and Testament in manner and form following;

Imprimis; I commend my Soul to Almighty God who gave it to me, and my body to the Earth from whence it came in hopes of a joyful Resurrection through my Lord and Savior Jesus Christ. And as for what worldly estate wherewith it hath pleased God to bless me I dispose thereof as follows;

Item. I give and bequeath unto six of my sons namely, Macclan, Jabez, Enoch, Ephraim, Elijah and Samuel all of my land that I am now possessed with, namely five hundred and forty five acres being apart of a tract called 'Athol', and one hundred acres being part of a tract called 'Hector's Hopyard' which said two parcels of land contain six hundred and forty five acres lyeth in Baltimore County aforesaid, and it is my Will and Desire that no part of the said six hundred and forty five acres of land be sold to any Stranger, by any or all of my sons, but yet my said sons may buy and sell of and to each other. The said six hundred and forty five acres to be divided in six equal parts and quality.

Item. I give and bequeath unto my eldest son John the sum of ten pounds sterling, or a warrant for two hundred acres of land to be paid him by and at the choice of my Executors hereafter named.

Item. I give and bequeath unto my said six sons namely, Macclan, Jabez, Enoch, Ephraim, Elijah and Samuel and unto my two daughters namely Kerenhappuch Hamilton and Sarah Bailey all my personal estate of what nature and kind soever to be equally and evenly divided between the said eight of my children.

Lastly I appoint my sons Macclan Bailey and Jabez Bailey to be my Executors of this my last Will and Testament, in witness whereof I the said George Bailey have hereunto set my hand and seal the day and year above written.

Witnesses;   George Bailey (Seal)
  Oliver Cromwell
  Cooper Oram
  James Hood

Will of GEORGE BAILEY (Continued)

On August 29, 1754 came Oliver Cromwell being one of the people called Quakers solemnly and sincerely testified and declared, and Cooper Oram one of the subscribing witnesses to the written Will and made oath on the Holy Evangelist of Almighty God that they saw the Testator George Bailey seal the within Will and heard him publish and declare the same to be his last Will and Testament, but did not see him stamp his name thereto, it being put thereto before the Deponents came to witness the said Will and that the said Testator acknowledged the name of George Bailey to be his stamp, and put thereto by himself, and that at the time of his sealing the said Will he was to the best of their apprehensions of sound and disposing mind and memory and that they subscribed their respective names as witnesses to the said Will in the presence of said Testator and at his request, and that they also saw James Hood, the other subscriber witness to the said Will, subscribe his name as an evidence thereto in the presence of said Testator and at his request.

Sworn before
Benj. Tasker,
Com. General.

(ATHOL, the plantation mentioned in this Will was located on the north side of the Patapsco River near Davis Run, toward Maidens Choice Run. Land Records W. D. pp 103.)

Issue of JOB & Elizabeth Ford.
(B-1)

FORD

(D1)   b. April 12, 1698   d.   June, 1749
m. Sept. 21, 1721   Margaret Farmer
(of Gregory & Sarah Hughes)
b.   Sept. 2, 1706   d.
(Issue; 5 sons & 6 daughters.)

JOB

(D2)   b. Dec. 20, 1701   d.   Nov. 11, 1739
m. Oct. 11, 1722   Constance West
(of Robert West)
b. April 20, 1703   d.
(Issue; 3 sons & 5 daughters.)

Widow married Sept., 1740 Joseph
Morgan.
Issue; 1 son, JOSEPH,
b.   Feb. 3, 1741

JAMES

(D3)   b. Mar. 26, 1704   d.   1745
m. Mar. 27, 1726   Bethiah Loney
(Issue; 5 sons & 4 daughters.)

Widow married Thomas Scarlett before 1750.

Ford undoubtedly was born in Anne Arundel Co. as were his other brothers, and at an early age they were taken by their mother to live on the tract called 'Repulta', however when Ford grew into manhood he decided to push farther up the Susequehanna River for we find that on Aug. 9, 1725 he Patented 60 acres of land known as 'Barnes Delight'. This land cost him three pounds and seven shillings sterling, and he was assessed a rent (or Tax) of two shillings and five pence per annum thereon.

He also purchased 43 acres adjoining this land for fifteen hundred pounds of tobacco, the tract being known as 'Barnes Neglect'.

These properties were located in what is now Harford County, opposite the place still known as the Bald Friar, or 'Upper Ferry'.

"Barnes Delight surveyed for Ford Barnes Sep. 15, 1725 lies on the west side of the Susequehanna River 'beginning at a bounded white oak at the head of a branch decending into the ford bottom'. The 'ford bottom' alluded to in the above certificate of survey was the river valley or bottom adjacent to the Bald Friar ford."

"The name proves that the ford was known by the English as early as 1721".

(Maryland Historical Magazine, Vol. 16, pp. 252; 1921—William B. Marye**)

Ford also acquired 'Dooley's (or Dewley's) Beginning', containing 100 acres and lying on the west side of the Susquehanna River north of Deer Creek and near Cabin Branch. On this land he was assessed a rent (or tax) of four shillings per year.

Although Ford died at the age of 51, he had in his lifetime accumulated considerable property as is shown by his Will and Inventory which follows;

"In the name of God Amen. I Ford Barnes of Baltimore County in the Province of Maryland being sick and weak in body but of perfect mind and memory, Blessed be God for the same and calling to mind the uncertainty of this Life do declare this to be my last will and testament in manner and form as followeth. Into the hands of Almighty God I do commit my Spirit and my body to the earth to be buried by my loving wife Margaret Barnes.

Item. I give unto my loving wife after all my just debts are paid, one third of my personal estate and my dwelling plantation during her natural life and the two other thirds of my personal estate to be divided between my six loving children, James, Elizabeth, Gregory, Ann, Margaret, and Martha Barnes, not forgetting my son Ford Barnes and my daughter Hanna Mitchell having given as much already as my circumstances will permit or afford.

Item. I give my loving son Ford Barnes the plantation he now lives on with seventy acres adjoining to it being part of a tract of land called and known by the name of 'Repulta' which said land I give to him and the heirs of his body lawfully begotten.

Item. I give unto my loving son James Barnes a tract of land called and known by the name of Barnes Delight and Neglect together which said land I give to him, his heirs and assigns forever.

Item. I give unto my loving son Gregory Barnes a tract of land called and known by the name of Dewley's Beginning, lying on the north side of Deer Creek which said land I give to him and his heirs and assigns forever.

Item. I give unto my loving wife Margaret Barnes a negro woman named Dutches during her natural life and after my wife decease to decend to my loving daughter Martha Barnes.

Item. I give to my loving son Ford Barnes my dwelling plantation after my wife decease, to him and the heirs of his body lawfully begotten.

Item. I give unto my loving son James Barnes one bay mare named Nancy, and her first living colt I give to my son Gregory Barnes.

Item. I give to my loving son Ford Barnes one half of the orchard on my dwelling plantation.

Item. I give unto my loving daughter Hannah Mitchell one ewe and a lamb.

Lastly, I nominate and appoint my dear beloved wife my whole and sole executrix and as a farther Testimony hereof have hereunto these presents put my hand and seal this second day of September A. D. 1748

(his)
FORD X BARNES.
(mark)

Signed sealed published and
declared this my last Will
and Testament.

Witnesses;   Rich'd Johns
              Philip Gover
              George Hargrove.

(Recorded Liber 26; pp119—Probated Jun. 25, 1749)

In his inventory filed May 5, 1750 by his wife Margaret, in addition to numerous items of personal property is mentioned the sum of 195 pounds, 1 shilling and 10½ pence Sterling.
(Recorded Liber 28, folio 163.)

JOB BARNES

Job owned 'Brothers Discovery' recorded Feb. 18, 1722, Land Records H W S-M 9; and Robert West deeded to his daughter Constance, Job's wife, as a 'gift' 100 acres, recorded I S-G 94, also 'Maidens Mount', recorded H W S-M 9.

'Maidens Mount' was surveyed for Robert West, Jan. 10, 1721 and is thus described; 'lying on the west side of the Susquehanna River beginning at four bounded beeches in the ford bottom of the said River near the mouth of a small branch'.

His inventory was filed Apl. 2, 1740, Liber 24, folio 509 and mentions the sum of 143 pounds and 15 shillings Sterling'.

An additional inventory was filed Nov. 17, 1740 showing 36 pounds and 10 pence.

JAMES BARNES

James owned 'Adam the First' a tract containing 103 acres. Recorded T R- A 210.

His inventory filed Oct. 25, 1747, Liber 44, folio 50, mentions 260 pounds, 7 shillings and 6½ pence Sterling.

Issue of GEORGE & Sarah Maclane.
(B-2)

JOHN (D4) (Owned) 'Hunting Ridge', Balto. Co. now Balto. City.)	b. m. b.	d. Helen Newsome d.	1789 (Nussum) 1801
MACLANE	b.	d.	1765
KERENHAPPUCH	b. Oct. 3, 1728 d. m. (Issue; WILLIAM)	——— Hamilton	
JABEZ	b.	d.	1769
ENOCH (D7)	b. m.	d. Kerenhappuch ———	1766
EPHRAIM	b.	d.	
ELIJAH	b. June 20, 1736 d.		
SAMUEL	b.	d.	1772
SARAH	b.	d.	

(The writer has no assurance that these names are in the proper order of birth, as the information has been taken from the Will of George Bailey.)

Will of ENOCH BAILEY.   Mar. 17, 1766.

Maryland ss. In the name of God, Amen. I Enoch Bailey of Baltimore County in the Province of Maryland being weak and low but of sound and perfect memory and mind do make this my last Will and Testament in manner and form following; revoking and by these presents annulling all other Wills heretofore made and done, and I do declare and publish this to be my last Will and Testament.

First, I commend my soul to Almighty God my Creator which in his Fatherly Goódness gave me nothing doubting that in his Infinite Goodness and mercy through the only merrits of my Savior and Redeemer Jesus Christ and he will receive it into Glory.

Secondly, my body I give to my mother Earth from whence it came and to be decently interred therein according to the will of my Executors hereinafter named.

Thirdly, as to the estate it hath pleased the Almighty to bless me with I give and dispose of it as follows;

Item. I give and bequeath to my three sons Joseph Bailey, Ephraim Bailey and William Bailey four hundred acres of land part of Butlers Farme and eighty three acres part of Fredrexsteed Inlarged and fifteen acres which I took up called Small Hope, to be equally divided in quantity and quality among my three sons and their heirs forever and if there should be occasion to sell anything to pay my debts, my will and desire is that eighty three acres part of Fredrexsteed Inlarged and fifteen acres called Small Hope be sold and the money applied toward discharging my debts by my Executors hereinafter named.

Item. I give and bequeath to my dear and well beloved wife Kerenhappuch Bailey One mollatto Boy named William to her and her heirs forever, and to my daughter Sarah Bailey One Negro Boy named Juba to her and her heirs forever.

Item. My will and desire is that all my just debts be paid and satisfied and the remainder of my estate be equally divided among my children male and female, and Lastly it is my will and desire that my brother John Murray be executor with my wife of this my last Will and Testament and I do hereby nominate and appoint them as such in witness whereof I have set my hand and affixed my seal this seventh day of March in the year seventeen hundred sixty six.

ENOCH BAILEY   (Seal)

Witnesses;
Jas. Calder
Shad Murray
John Oram.   Probated Apl. 29, 1766

Issue of FORD & Margaret Farmer.
(C·1)

FORD	(E1)	b. June 26, 1724 d. June 29, 1761 m. Oct. 20, 1743 Ruth Garrett (of Bennett & Arabella) b. May 21, 1729 d. (Five sons & two daughters.)
JAMES		b. June 7, 1726 d. Mar. 27, 1729
HANNAH	(E2)	b. Sept. 26, 1728 d. m. Kent Mitchell (of Thomas & Ann) b. Jan. 2, 1724 d. 1797 (Two sons & three daughters.)
JAMES	(E3)	b. Jan. 5, 1730 d. 1804 m. Sophia Osborn
ELIZABETH		b. Jan. 26, 1732 d. Mar. 22, 1810 m. Feb. 25, 1749 Solomon Armstrong
GREGORY FARMER*	(E4)	b. Jan. 21, 1734 d. Mar. 27, 1808 m. Nov. 30, 1758 Elizabeth Mitchell* (of Richard & Elizabeth) b. June 16, 1739 d. April 18, 1832
ANN		b. Mar. 31, 1737 d.
MARGARET	(E5)	b. Feb. 26, 1738 d. m. Feb. 20, 1757 Joshua Armstrong
MARTHA		b. June 8, 1742 d. Oct. 12, 1742
MARTHA		b. Jan. 1, 1743 d.
JOB		b. Mar. 5, 1747 d. before 1749

Will of FORD BARNES, May 24, 1761.

I Ford Barnes of Baltimore County in Maryland do make and ordain this my last Will and Testament, In manner and form following;

Imprimis; It is my will and desire that as soon as conveniently can be after my decease my Executrix hereafter named, Pay all my just Debts.

Item. I give and bequeath unto my loving wife Ruth Barnes the use of my plantation, on my tract of land called Repulta during and until my son Bennett arrives at the age of twenty-one years and use of one-third part of the land aforesaid on which plantation she may see best to live at during her natural life and not to be molested or disturbed therein.

Item. I give and bequeath unto my son Richard Barnes One acre of land out of my tract of land called Repulta, out of that part of the said tract that is taken in as surplus land of the same, to be lain off by his brother·Bennett Barnes, when he may arrive at the age of twenty-one years, or any part of the said surplus land the said Bennett may see proper above the first turning of the run from the River Susquehanna that runs through the said land, which said One acre of land to be lain off as aforesaid, I give unto my said son Richard Barnes, to him my said son Richard and the heirs of his body lawfully begotten forever.

Item. I give and bequeath unto my son Amos Barnes One acre of land out of my tract of land called Repulta, out of that part of the said tract that is taken in as surplus land of the same to be lain off by his brother Bennett Barnes, when he may arrive at the age of twenty-one years on any part of the said surplus land the said Bennett may see proper above the first turning of the run from the River Susquehanna that runs through the said land which said one acre of land to be lain off as aforesaid, I give unto my said son Amos Barnes, to him my said son Amos and the heirs of his body lawfully begotten forever.

Item. I give and bequeath unto my son Bennett Barnes all the remaining part of my tract of land called Repulta that has not been above divided unto my sons Richard & Amos, which said tract of land called Repulta I give and bequeath unto my said son Bennett Barnes, and to the heirs of his body lawfully begotten forever.

Item. It is my will and desire that my three sons Bennett, Richard and Amos after they have got schooling sufficient which I leave to the discretion of their Guardian by me appointed and hereafter named, be bound out to such trades as their Guardian may see most proper for them, and there to continue until they respectively arrive at the age of twenty-one years.

Item. I give my loving wife Ruth Barnes, one full third part of my personal estate after my just debts are paid.

Item. It is my will and desire that all the residue of my estate be equally divided between my four children, namely Bennett, Richard, Arabella & Amos.

Item. I hereby appoint my Brother in Law, Amos Garrett, Guardian of my children. Willing and deserving my said Brother in Law, to see my sons educated in a proper manner for the business he my Trustee & Friend may see proper to put them to when they arrive to proper age to be bound out, and I hereby further Impower my said friend Amos Garrett if he should see his sister, my said wife Ruth Barnes to neglect the education of my said sons to enter on and rent out two-thirds of my plantation or land called Repulta and with the rent thereof to educate my said sons till they have arrived at the ages to be bound out to trades as a/fd, and I also will that in case my said wife should marry again a person that my said Trustee and Friend should suspect would not take proper care of my said children or their parts of my estate appertaining to them, that in such case, my said Trustee and Friend, Amos Garrett to take out of his said sisters said hands my said children and the parts of my estate appertaining to them, and its farther my will that in case of the death of my said Brother in Law Amos Garrett before my said sons are bound out to their respective trades that in such case it is my will and desire that my brother Gregory Barnes see my children educated and bound out to trades as soon as they arrive to proper ages.

Item. It is my will and desire that my beloved wife Ruth Barnes have the full use of my personal estate during her natural life except as before devised my said Brother in Law Amos Garrett should see cause to call my children's part of my estate out of her hands.

Lastly, I hereby appoint my loving wife Ruth Barnes my executrix of this my last Will requesting my Brother in Law Amos Garrett to assist her in the settling the amounts due to and from my estate.

IN WITNESS, that the Foregoing is my last Will, I hereby revoke all other Wills by me heretofore made, and have to this present sett my hand this twenty-fourth day of May, in the year of our Lord Seventeen Hundred & Sixty One.

FORD BARNES.

Witnesses;
Benj. Culver
Joseph Bailey
Elizabeth Cord

CODICIL TO ABOVE WILL.

Whereas I Ford Barnes of Baltimore County have heretofore made and subscribed my last Will and Testament, but have thought it advisable to make this present Codicil thereto, If my loving wife Ruth Barnes should prove with child, in such case I will and bequeath unto the said child to be born of my said wife if she should prove with child, if a son, one acre of land out of my tract of land called Repulta to be lain off by my son Bennett Barnes adjoining the acre to be lain off for my son Richard Barnes, which said acre of land to be lain off as aforesaid, I give and bequeath unto the child my said wife now goes with (if proves a son) unto him and the heirs of his body lawfully begotten forever, and I also will and desire that the child my said wife now goes with if she proves with child an equal part of my personal estate with the rest of my children.

IN WITNESS whereof I have hereto sett my hand this twenty-first day of June, Anno. Dom. Seventeen Hundred & Sixty One.

FORD BARNES.

Witnesses;
James Barnes
Ann Williams
Margaret Armstrong.

Probated Dec. 31, 1761.

From WILL OF JAMES BARNES.

To wife Sophia one third of personal property and profit on two tracts of land to go to the two daughters when 16 yrs of age.

To daughter ELIZABETH ORSBERN 17£ 10s

To daughter MARGARET the tract of land purchased from Ben Everist when she becomes 16 years

To daughter MARY when she becomes 16 the tract of land on south/w side of Swan Creek Rd known as Judds place, and to be conveyed by John Hanson. If she should die before 16 yrs survivor to inherit. Remainder to be equally divided between Margaret and Mary and my step children Sarah Cole, and Benj. Cole.

Executor Aquila Mitchell.

his

James X Barnes

mark

Witnesses;
Wm. Maxwell
John Mahan, Jr.
James Horner

Made Aug 27 1803

Issue of JOB & Constance West.
(C-1)

JOB	(E6)	b.	Dec. 20, 1723	d.	
		m.	Feb. 2, 1749	Mary Crawford	
		b.		d.	1800
MARGARET		b.	July 30, 1725	d.	
JOHN		b.	Feb. 2, 1727	d.	
ELIZABETH		b.	Mar. 2, 1730	d.	Aug. 23, 1734
CASSIAH		b.	Oct. 27, 1732	d.	
ELIZABETH		b.	Aug. 23, 1735	d.	
THOMAS		b.	Sept. 27, 1737	d.	
CONSTANCE		b.	Sept. 30, 1739	d.	

From WILL
of
MARY (CRAWFORD) BARNES
Made Dec. 29, 1799.

To daughter RACHEL 2 s 6 d of my third part of personal property.
To daughter RUTH the same.
To daughter SARAH the same.
Remainder to daughter HANNAH for services during sickness.

                                   MARY N. BARNES.

Witnesses;
Jas. Fisher
Robert Morgan
An. Nevill

Issue of JAMES & Bethiah Loney.
(C-1)

JOHN	(E9)	b. Nov. 24, 1727 d. 1767
		m. Aug. 10, 1749 Elizabeth Scott (?)
JEMIMA	(E10)	b. May 5, 1729 d.
		m. Feb. 19, 1747 Sam'l. Kimball
		b. June 27, 1725 d.
JAMES		b. April 4, 1732 d.
RACHEL	(E12)	b. June 4, 1734 d.
		m. April 18, 1751 Robert Crate
		b. d. Mar. 31, 1761
		(After husband's death Widow married June 21, 1762 William Steavenson)
WILLIAM		b. Nov. 17, 1736 d.
RICHARD & MARY		b. June 1, 1740 d.
FORD		b. Sept. 11, 1743 d.
BOTHIA		b. Feb.11, 1745-6 d.

Issue of JOHN & Helen Newsome (Nussum).
(C-2)

MARY   b.   April 5, 1740   d.

SARAH   (E15)   b. Feb. 24, 1741-2   d.
                      m.   1765   JOHN CALVERT
                      (de jure Eighth Lord Baltimore)
                      b.   1742   d.   1790

ELAM   b. Feb. 24, 1741-2   d.

HELLEN   (E15)   b.   d.
                      m.   1772   JOHN CALVERT
                      (de jure Eighth Lord Baltimore)
                      b.   1742   d.   1790

GEORGE   b.   d.

JOHN NEWSOME   b.   d.   1801

ELIZABETH   b.   d.
                      m.   —————— Parker.

(Names may not be in order of birth as same were taken from the Will of
JOHN BAILEY.)

Issue of ENOCH & Kerenhappuch ————.
(C-2)

JOSEPH   (E16)   b.   d.
                             m. Dec. 27, 1748 Margaret Osborn
                             b. Mar. 13, 1727 d.
                             (of Benjamin & Sarah)

                           (Issue; Five sons and two daughters.)

(From Md. Hist. Magazine, Vol. 26; pp262-3,
Registered sloop 'Vigilant' 40 tons, May 13, 1748
                                 Joseph Bailey, Master.

From Vol. 26; pp349, registered sloop 'Prudent Mary', 15 tons, May 6, 1749.
                                 Joseph Bailey, Master.
              Joseph Bailey and Levin Hodson, Owners.)

EPHRAIM   b.   d.

WILLIAM   b.   d.

SARAH   b.   d.

(Names may not be in order of birth, same taken from Will of ENOCH
BAILEY.)

    Referring to the past records we have reason to believe that this family
first settled in Baltimore County in the neighborhood or near what is now
Catonsville.

    Reference B-2a states that George Bailey was appointed road overseer
'from the Soldiers Delight to the landing at the head of the Patapsco'. (Soldiers Delight is located about one mile north of Harrisonville, Baltimore
County, which is on the Liberty Road out of Baltimore City.)

In this same reference we also find that George Bailey was appointed road overseer 'from the main falls by Christopher Randall's to Gwins Falls . . . ' and further the opinion states that this was in all probability 'The Old Frederick Road' by Ellicott Upper Mills (Ellicott City).

We also find in B-2c that the plantation owned by George Bailey called 'Athol' was located on the North side of the Patapsco River near Davis Run &c, a more modern description being, south of Old Frederick Road, between or perhaps including Irvington and Ten Hills in Baltimore, and his son John owned Hunting Ridge located on north side of Edmondson Ave., opposite Ten Hills, also in Baltimore (Md.).

At this period of the record (D-7) we find Joseph Bailey as a waterman, having owned one sloop and part owner in another, and undoubtedly in sailing the Chesapeake he landed at the head of the Bay where he met and married Margaret Osborn, whose parents lived at Swan Creek (now Harford County).

Joseph was the fore-father of the Baileys who later resided in Harford County (Md.). Margaret Osborn's grandfather, William Osborn, immigrated from England in 1664 and later operated a ferry across Bush River. The following is an interesting epistle concerning the life and some of the experiences of this man.

Copy of a letter written by Dr. George Hays, of Aberdeen, Md., in 1875 to Rev. George A. Leakin of Baltimore.

'The first house built in Harford County was at Old Baltimore by William Osborn on Old House Point, and in the old grave yard his body rests, the burial of the first white man.

Osborn was a younger son, his family is as old as the present dynasty of England. The Osborns led the Danes against William the Conqueror, they formed an alliance and Osborn with his family were to have a perpetual annuity. This the heirs still receive and Osborn Place is still the abode of the Royal Family.

This I had from my Grand-mother Hollis whose maiden name was Sarah Osborn and from my Great Aunt Fanny Osborn and history confirms it. Fanny Osborn often thrilled me, when a child, with Osborn's adventures with Indians (Susquehannocks) who in one of their raids stole his eldest son. He and his retainers followed the Indians across the Bay but failed to recover him. This boy whom he never saw again, was kindly treated by his captors and an old chief, before his father died, told him his son was living and had become a great chief among the red men. He subsequently was one of those chiefs who signed the treaty with William Penn in 1682. The father never recovered from the loss of his boy but died of a broken heart.'

HOSEA or Hosur   (F2)   b.   d.
m. June 10, 1788   Mary Wood
m. Jan.   8, 1809   Eliz. Lester
m. Mar. 26, 1812   Mary Garretson

(The record of these three marriages are recorded in St. Georges Parrish Register. The writer is not certain that the same Hosea Barnes married all three of the wives but it looks like it was the same man, inasmuch as the marriages are so close together.)

Issue of FORD & Ruth Garrett.
(D-1)

FORD   b.   Sept. 7, 1749   d.   April 8, 1761

CASSANDRA   b.   Feb. 17, 1751   d. young

BENNETT   (F1)   b. Sept. 17, 1753   d. June 15, 1826
                        m.   Esther
                        b.   1757   d. April 30, 1829

ARABELLA   b.   Jan. 17, 1755   d.
                        m.   Feb. 1, 1796   James Young

RICHARD   b.   Nov. 5, 1757   d.
                        m. Jan. 17, 1783   Sarah Kidd

AMOS   (F3)   b. Nov. 17, 1759   d.   1797
                        m.   Rebecca Wood
                        (of John)

FORD   b.   Jan. 24, 1761   d.   Sept. 9, 1800
                        m. Nov. 30, 1792   Ann Gilmore

WILL OF AMOS BARNES.

In the name of God, Amen. I Amos Barnes of Harford County and State of Maryland, being weak in body but of sound memory, blessed be God, do this fifth day of September in the year of our Lord, One thousand seven hundred and ninety-seven, make and publish this my last will and testament in manner following;

After all my just debts and funeral charges are paid;

I give to my eldest son John Barnes, one negro boy names Isaac. Also to my son Garrett Barnes, one negro boy named Ben and to my daughter Sarah Barnes, one negro boy named Bill.

Then I will all the remaining part of my estate, both real and personal shall be valued and divided into three equal parts and then be divided equally between my three children in the following manner;

First I will that my lot of ground which is part of a tract of land called Repulta, be divided by a line beginning forty feet west of the west side of my brother Ford Barnes present stone dwelling house and to be run parallel with west end of the whole lot.

Then I will that my eldest son John Barnes shall have that part of the lot lays on and joins the river Susquehanna, except a road twelve feet wide which shall be kept open for the use of both lots to the aforesaid river. But in case that part which I give to my son John Barnes should be valued to more than one-third part of my whole estate, then he shall pay to the other two, as they arrive at age, as much as will make their part equal to his part.

Then I will that my son Garrett Barnes shall have the west end of the whole lot from the line drawn 40 feet west of the west side of my brother Ford Barnes present stone dwelling house which divides the whole lot into two parts, with the privilege of the aforesaid twelve feet road to the river, and in case his part of the whole lot shall be valued to more than one-third part of my whole estate, then he shall pay to the deficient so as to make them equal.

Then I will to my daughter Sarah Barnes out of the remaining part of my estate as much as shall make her part equal to one-third of my estate, after settled up, shall be put to use and that the income arising from said estate shall be to the education and maintenance of my two sons and daughter till they arrive at age, the management of which I leave to my brother Bennett Barnes and to my friend John Michael, who I leave as my executors of this my last will and testament, in witness whereof I, Amos Barnes have set my hand and seal this day and year above written.

Amos Barnes.

2-67

Witness;
Hosur Barnes
John Michael
Joshua Wood

Issue of Kent & HANNAH BARNES.
(D-1)

WILLIAM	b. Aug. 12, 1747	d.
SARAH	b. Mar. 5, 1749	d.
JAMES	b. June 5, 1752	d.
SUSANNA	b. Aug. 12, 1754	d.
SOPHIA	b. Feb. 20, 1758	d.

Issue of JAMES & Sophia Osborn
(D-1)

ELIZABETH OSBORN	b.	d.
MARGARET	b.	d.
MARY	b.	d.

Issue of GREGORY FARMER* & Elizabeth Mitchell*
(D-1)

AVARILLA	(F8)	b. Dec. 16, 1759	d. 1846
		m. June 20, 1776	JOSIAH BAILEY
		(of Joseph & Margaret Osborn)	
		b. Sept. 28, 1749	d. 1843
FORD	(F5)	b. April 4, 1761	d. Feb. 5, 1798
		m. Jan. 24, 1788	Mary Gilbert
RICHARD Sr.*	(F6)	b. June 25, 1762	d. Nov. 29, 1830
		m. Dec. 19, 1782	Sarah Gilbert*
		b. Aug. 28, 1762	d. Feb. 13, 1811
		m. Feb. 25, 1812	Mary Bayless
		b. Oct. 4, 1767	d. Dec. 8, 1848
		(No issue)	
RACHEL*	(F9)	b. Mar. 23, 1764	d. April 27, 1850
		m. June 10, 1787	AQUILA BAILEY
		(of Joseph & Margaret Osborn)	
		b. Nov. 7, 1756	d. Aug. 31, 1810
GREGORY*		b. Dec. 17, 1765	d. Nov. 26, 1846
		m. Jan. 6, 1788	Elizabeth Osborn
		(No issue)	
	(F7)	m.	Elizabeth Hawkins
		(of Richard & Avarilla)	
		b. Sept. 8, 1775	d. April 28, 1859
MARY		b. June 14, 1767	d.
		m.	William Maxwell
SARAH	(F10)	b. Mar. 6, 1769	d.
		m.	Thomas Coen
		b.	d.
FARMER		b. April 25, 1772	d.
		(Went West)	
JOHN		b. May 5, 1774	d. 1778
ARABELLA	(F13)	b. Dec. 6, 1775	d. Mar. 12, 1810
		m.	James Thomas
ELIZABETH		b. Aug. 30, 1778	d.
		m.	Robert Curry
ANN		b. April 4, 1782	d.
		m.	Moses Curry

WILL of RICHARD BARNS, Sr.

In the name of God, Amen, I, Richard Barns of Harford County in the state of Maryland, being in perfect health of body and of sound disposing mind and memory and understanding, considering the certainty of death and the uncertainty of the time thereof, being desirious to settle my world-ly affairs and thereby be the better prepared to leave this world when it shall please God to call me hence, do hereby make and publish this my last will and testament in manner and form as following, that is to say, first and principally, I commit my soul into the hands of Almighty God and my body to the earth to be decently buried at the discretion of my exec-utor herein mentioned, and after my debts and funeral charges are paid and my wifes third taken out, I devise and bequeath as follows:

Item: I give and bequeath unto my son Mordecai G. Barns all that part of my land whereon he now lives, known by the name of Middlemores Angles, with all the improvements and appurtenances thereon and thereto belonging, containing thirty-five (35) acres more or less, lying on the west side of two stones set up and marked R. B. 1829 1-2, between him and his brother Richard Barnes, to him the said Mordecai G. Barns and his heirs forever.

Item: I give and bequeath unto my son Richard Barns 89¾ acres more or less called Beedles Reserve, Scotchmans Generosity and St. Martins Lud-gate, the plantation whereon I now live, with all buildings and other im-provements thereon and thereby belonging, to him and his lawful heirs forever.

Item: I give and bequeath to my son Richard Barns, one bay horse called Liberty, one black horse Peter, one yoke of oxen, two milk cows, first choice of four sheep, one sow, one feather bed bedstead and furniture, one sideboard, one case of drawers black walnut, one walnut table, one musket, six chairs and all the farming implements to me belonging, to him and his heirs forever.

Item: I give and bequeath to my beloved wife Mary Barns in addition to her one-third, one bay colt rising two years old to her and heirs for-ever.

Item: To my niece Mary Coen one milk cow and two sheep.

Item: To my grandson Charles L. Bailey, one feather bed, bed stead and furniture.

I devise and bequeath the rest and residue of my property (personal) to be equally divided between my two Mordecai G. Barns and Richard Barns and their heirs forever.

And lastly I do hereby constitute and appoint my beloved wife Mary Barns and my son Richard Barns sole executors of my last will and testament. In witness whereof I, the said testator do make and ordain this my last will and testament annulling all former wills made by me. Signed, sealed, published and pronounced by the said Richard Barns in the year of our Lord one thousand, eight hundred and thirty, in the presence of us.

                              Signed Richard Barns

Witness:
John Coen
Aquilla Treadway
Thomas Mitchell

Probated December 30, 1830.
Fol.1,pp 522.

Issue of Joshua & MARGARET BARNES.
(D-1)

SOLOMON   b.   May 7, 1758   d.

Issue of JOB & Mary Crawford.
(D-2)

JOB	b. June 11, 1752		d.
RACHEL	b. Aug. 13, 1754		d.
EZEKIEL	b. July 4, 1758		d.
MARY	b.		d.
RUTH	b.		d.
	m.		Amos Silver
	b.	1760	d.
SARAH	b.		d. Mar. 26, 1815
	m.		David Silver
	b.	1767	
HANNAH	b.		d.

(Preston's History of Harford County, Md., lists Job and Ezekiel Barnes as having enlisted Apl. 1, 1776, as privates in Capt. John Patrick's Co. No. 17, Revolutionary War. No doubt the above mentioned are those referred to.)

Issue of JOHN & Elizabeth Scott ?
(D-3)

ELIZABETH	b.	Dec. 4, 1761	d.

She married and gave issue to
seven children.
Husband's name unknown.

Issue of Samuel & JEMIMA BARNES.
(D-3)

ANN	b.	Oct. 1, 1747	d. young
RACHEL	b.	Jan. 9, 1749	d.
JAMES	b.	Mar. 22, 1751	d.
	(un-married)		
BETHYA	b.	May 4, 1753	d.
HANNAH	b.	Dec. 11, 1755	d.
JEMIMA	b.	Aug. 9, 1758	d.

Kimball married a second time to Sarah ————. His Will (1786)
mentions all the above named children, except Ann, and also the following;

ZACHARIAH	b.	1773	d. in Maryland
SUSAN COWAN	b.		d. in Ohio
	m.		William Hamby
ELIJAH	b.	1779	d. in Ohio
	m.		Mary Stephenson
NANNY	b.		d.
SEMELA	b.		d.

Issue of Robert & RACHEL BARNES.
(D-3)

REBECCA	b. Nov. 24, 1752 d.
SARAH	b. Feb. 17, 1755 d.
RICHARD	b. Mar. 19, 1757 d.
FRANCIS	b. April 15, 1759 d.
CORDELIA	b. April 21, 1761 d.

Issue of William & RACHEL BARNES.
(D-3)

GEORGE	b. Mar. 28, 1763 d.
WILLIAM	b. Feb. 14, 1765 d.
JAMES	b. d.

Issue of John (de jure Eighth Lord Baltimore) & SARAH BAILEY.
(D-4)

CECILIUS	b. Dec. 29, 1767 d.
HENRIETTA	b.　　　　1769 d. m.　　　　———— Birch (No issue)

Issue of John & HELLEN BAILEY.
(D-4)

SARAH	b.　　　　1774 d. m.　　　　1803 John Heaton (No issue)
ANNE	b.　　　　1776 d.　　　　1848 m.　　　　1799 Capt. David J. Coxe (No issue)
ELIZABETH	b. Feb. 21, 1777 d. Dec. 15, 1833 m. Jan.　7, 1802 Dr. Jos. Nicklin
HANNAH	b.　　　　1778 d.　　　　1861 m.　　　　1793 John Jett
DELIA	b.　　　　1780 d.　　　　1873 (Un-married)
GETTIE	b.　　　　1785 d.　　　　1816 m.　　　　1801 Gabriel Smither

Issue of JOSEPH & Margaret Osborn.
(D-7)

JOSIAH*	(F8)	b. Sept. 28, 1749 d. Dec. 1843 m. June 20, 1776 AVARILLA BARNES* (of Gregory & Eliz. Mitchell) b. Dec. 16, 1759 d. Mar. 1847
CHARLES		b. Nov. 17, 1754 d. (Un-married)
AQUILA "Revolutionary War"	(F9)	b. Nov. 7, 1756 d. Aug. 31, 1810 m. June 10, 1787 RACHEL BARNES* (of Gregory & Eliz. Mitchell) b. Mar. 23, 1764 d. April 27, 1850
BENEDICT	(F11)	b. Jan. 15, 1759 d. m. Mary Morgan.
SARAH		b. Oct. 8, 1761 d. m. John Wood
AVARILLA		b. d. (Un-married)
EZEKIEL		b. d.

Issue of BENNETT & Esther ————.
(E-1)

JOHN*　　　　　(G1)　b. April 10, 1788　d. Mar. 23, 1843
　　　　　　　　　　　　m.　　　　　　　　Widow Mitchell
　　　　　　　　　　　　　　　　　　　　　nee James.
　　　　　　　　　　　　(Mother of Harvey Mitchell)

ROBERT　　　　　　　b.　　　　　　　　d.

BENNETT　　　　(G3)　b.　　　　　　　　d.　　　　　1845

RICHARD　　　　(G4)　b.　　　　　　　　d.
　　　　　　　　　　　　m.　　　　　　　　Mary K. Myers
　　　　　　　　　　　　b. Aug. 15, 1787　d. April 27, 1868

HENRY §　　　　(G5)　b. Jan.　7, 1792　d.　Mar. 3, 1858
　　　　　　　　　　　　m. Aug. 29, 1822　Sarah B. Whitaker §
　　　　　　　　　　　　b. Oct. 26, 1793　d.　June 5, 1841
　　　　　　　　　　　　m. Sept. 9, 1841　Eliza Kenly §
　　　　　　　　　　　　b.　April 4, 1804　d.　Dec. 26, 1872
　　　　　　　　　　　　(of Samuel & Elizabeth Bayless)

REBECCA　　　　　　　b.　　　　　　　　d.
　　　　　　　　　　　　m.　　　　　　　　———— Evans

SARAH　　　　　　　　b.　　　　　　　　d.
　　　　　　　　　　　　m.　　　　　　　　———— Bailey

WILLIAM　　　　(G6)　b.　　　　　　　　d.
　　　　　　　　　　　　m.　　　　　　　　Caroline W. Donahoo §
　　　　　　　　　　　　b. Aug. 28, 1814　d.　Oct. 14, 1872

(It is not certain that this family is arranged in the proper order of birth.)

Will of JOHN BARNES

Made March 17, 1843.

I give and bequeath to my daughter Ellen Evans, wife of Wm. F. Evans of Harford Co., all that tract or parcel of land composed of part of two tracts called 'Cooks Rest' and 'Middlemores Angles', containing —— acres, more or less, being the same conveyed to me by Gregory Barnes by deed bearing date the twelfth day of January 1799 and recorded in liber ISG No. 0-429 land Records of Harford Co.

And I further will and devise that the said parcel of land that I have hereby devised to my daughter Ellen Evans, wife of William F. Evans, I only intend she shall have the use thereof with the power of devising and directing the management thereof and for that I will all the above described tract of land to John H. Mitchell and his heirs, in trust for the separate use of my said daughter Ellen during her life and after her death to the heirs of her body and if she dies without such heirs then to such person or persons as she may will and devise.

I devise and bequeath all the rest and residue of my estate, both real and personal to my beloved wife in fee simple, on condition that she cause to be paid at her death fifty dollars to each of my sisters, Rebecca Evans and Sarah Bailey.

And lastly I do hereby constitute John H. Mitchell sole executor of this my last will and testament, revolking and annulling all former wills by me heretofore made, ratifying and confirming this my last will and testament.

In testimony whereof I have hereunto set my hand and affixed my seal this 17th day of March in the year of our Lord 1843

Signed JOHN BARNES   (SEAL)

Witnesses;
Daniel Michael
Richard Mitchell
William Slee

Probated Apl. 4, 1843

From Will of BENNETT BARNES.

Made Dec. 31, 1844.

Negro man Stephen Pearson to be set free Jan. 1, 1847, negro girl Susan Pearson to be set free Jan. 1, 1855.

To Wife her lawful portion and rest equally divided among my children, THOMAS BENNETT BARNES, ELIZABETH HAUFMAN BARNES, WILLIAM HENRY BARNES, and JOHN ROBERT BARNES.

Issue of HOSEA & Mary Wood (?).
(E-0)

AMOS §	(G2)	b. July 5, 1792 d. Sept. 28, 1865	
		m. Ann Catherine ———§	
		b. about 1800 d. Jan. 26, 1858	

JOHN Lisby	b. Dec. 17, 1797 d.

JOSHUA WOOD	b. May 1, 1801 d.
	(May have died young ?)

REBECCA	b. d.

(There is some question as to the accuracy of this family. St. Georges Parish record gives the dates of births of John Lisby and Joshua Wood, and mentions parents' names as Hosea & Mary.

From the Will of MARY BARNES, made May 9, 1815 we have the following;

To son AMOS all money due me from Reuben Sutton ($200.) and one set silver tea spoons. To son JOHN two pieces of gold each $5.00 together with all old silver. Also my mare and interest on the Sutton Debt. To daughter REBECCA feather bed and furniture, one bureau, one red cow with white face, one set of silver tea spoons. Remainder to be divided equally between children. Son JOHN executor.

Witnesses; Richard Barnes
            Aquila Osborn)

Issue of AMOS & Rebecca Wood.
(E·1)

JOHN	(G7)	b.	d.	about 1816
		m. Mar. 19, 1812	Elizabeth Barnes?	

GARRETT	b.	d.

SARAH	b.	d.
	m.	Charles Toner (?)

From WILL OF JOHN BARNES of Amos.

Made Feb. 26, 1816

To wife Elizabeth, Negro man Sam and Negro girl Lydia.
All personal and Bible, also the plantation Stoney Ridge so long as she is in widowhood may remain in the place, she to have all stock and implements. Executor may sell or rent and pay wife her one-third.
To son BENNETT and child of which my wife is now pregnant, the following negroes;
Isaac, Ben, Naomy, Casandra and Harriot and their offspring. Should the children die before maturity the negroes to be set free.

JOHN BARNES.

Witness;
William Smith
Isaac Webster
John Dever.

Issue of FORD & Mary Gilbert.
(E-4)

SARAH

b. Jan. 24, 1796 d.
m.   JARRETT BAILEY
(of AQUILA & RACHEL BARNES.)
b. May 22, 1795 d.

(Issue; two children)

Issue of RICHARD Sr.* & Sarah Gilbert.*
(E-4)

WINSTON

b. Sept. 5, 1784 d. Aug. 12, 1796

MARY A.* (Polly)   (G15)

b. Sept. 7, 1787 d. Sept. 3, 1828
m. Mar. 3, 1808 ASAEL BAILEY
(of JOSIAH & AVARILLA BARNES)
b. Aug. 27, 1778 d. Sept. 21, 1825

MORDECAI GILBERT (G8)
(War of 1812-14
April 18-25, 1813 22nd Md. Militia.)

b. Aug. 13, 1791 d. April 30, 1866
m. Jan. 1, 1818 SARAH BAILEY
(of AQUILA & RACHEL BARNES)
b. Feb. 11, 1793 d. Aug. 23, 1873

ELIZABETH

b. June 16, 1795 d. Nov. 24, 1801

RICHARD Jr.*   (G9)

b. Jan. 24, 1805 d. Sept. 10, 1849
m. Jan. 24, 1832 Susanna Osborn*
b. June 4, 1808 d. Oct. 27, 1892

Issue of GREGORY & Elizabeth Hawkins.
(E-4)

BENNETT		b. July 10, 1794	d. in Balto.	
HARRIETT‡	(G19)	b. Dec. 24, 1796	d. Dec. 30, 1870	
		m. Dec. 24, 1818	John Bailey‡	
		(of Josiah & Avarilla Barnes)		
		b. Jan. 19, 1787	d. June 24, 1880	
RICHARD		b. Mar. 26, 1799	d.	
FORD	(G10)	b. Aug. 4, 1801	d.	
		m. Jan. 1, 1822	Mary A. Osborn**	
		b. Mar. 14, 1802	d. Mar. 4, 1880	
WILLIAM*		b. Mar. 24, 1804	d. June 18, 1872	
		(Un-married)		
JOHN HAWKINS¶	(G11)	b. Oct. 19, 1806	d. Jan. 26, 1889	
		m. Oct. 30, 1832	Ann Smith	
		b. May 31, 1807	d. Oct. 11, 1844	
		m.	Avarilla J. Fulton¶	
		b. Sept. 17, 1804	d. Jan. 28, 1879	
GREGORY FARMER		b. Feb. 1, 1809	d.	
ELIZABETH¶		b. Mar. 5, 1810	d. Nov. 25, 1887	
		(Un-married)		
MARY ANN‡	(G17)	b. Dec. 15, 1812	d. 1897	
		m. July 16, 1835	Shadrach Bailey‡	
		(of Josiah & Avarilla Barnes)		
		b. Sept. 10, 1782	d. 1868	
HOSEA¶	(G12)	b. Aug. 29, 1816	d. May 7, 1900	
		m. Dec. 15, 1840	Sarah Gilbert¶	
		(of Amos & Sarah Bailey)		
		b. Jan. 31, 1820	d. Mar. 13, 1903	
JAMES	(G13)	b. July 17, 1817	d. Mar. 29, 1901	
		m. Aug. 31, 1837	Mary A. Walter	
		(of Henry & Mary)		
		b. Oct. 2, 1812	d. Mar. 17, 1886	
ROBERT AMOS	(G14)	b. Jan. 19, 1821	d. July 12, 1898	
		m. May 28, 1846	Avarilla A. Gilbert	
		(of Amos & Sarah Bailey)		
		b. Aug. 24, 1823	d. July 14, 1916	

Issue of JOSIAH & AVARILLA BARNES.
(E-16; E-4)

ELIZABETH		b. Mar. 24, 1777 d. m. George Walker
ASAEL*	(G15)	b. Aug. 27, 1778 d. Sept. 21, 1825 m. Mar. 3, 1808 MARY A. BARNES (of Richard & Sarah Gilbert) b. Sept. 7, 1787 d. Sept. 3, 1828
SARAH	(G16)	b. May 10, 1780 d. Aug. 14, 1836 m. Jan. 19, 1804 Amos Gilbert b. April 16, 1774 d. Feb. 20, 1836
SHADRACH‡	(G17)	b. Sept. 10, 1782 d. 1868 m. July 16, 1835 MARY ANN BARNES‡ (of Gregory & Eliz. Hawkins) b. Dec. 15, 1812 d.
AQUILA†	(G18)	b. Oct. 29, 1784 d. Nov. 2, 1861 m. Martha Evans† b. 1784 d. Feb. 1, 1860
JOHN‡ (Private in Captain Jos. Perrigo's Co. of Inf., 41st Regiment (Hutchins) Md. Militia. Served Aug. 25, 1814 to Nov. 30, 1814.) (War 1812-14)	(G19)	b. Jan. 18, 1787 d. June 24, 1880 m. Dec. 24, 1818 HARRIETT BARNES‡ (of Gregory & Eliz. Hawkins) b. Dec. 24, 1796 d. Dec. 30, 1870
AVARILLA		b. Jan. 20, 1791 d. Mar. 31, 1871 m. 1822 Cyrus Courtney b. May 23, 1790 d. Nov. 30, 1859
JOSIAH		b. Feb. 16, 1795 d. m. Catherine Vandegrift
CHARLES	(G21)	b. Jan. 7, 1797 d. Feb. 3, 1869 m. Oct. 7, 1832 Deborah Pinkney b. July 28, 1812 d. April 17, 1899
MARY		b. Dec. 26, 1798 d. m. Rev. Jacob James

Issue of AQUILA & RACHEL BARNES.
(E-16; E-4)

WILLIAM LLOYD	(G23)	b. Mar. 23, 1788	d. Aug. 25, 1863
		m. May 5, 1814	Amelia Holaday
		b.	d. Mar. 4, 1830
		(of Baltimore, Md.)	
		m. Nov. 10, 1830	Jerusha Harvey
		b. Dec. 5, 1807	d. Aug. 5, 1882
		(of Baltimore, Md.)	
EVAN		b. April 23, 1789	d. Sept. 5, 1801
MARY		b. Oct. 7, 1790	d. June 4, 1794
ELIZABETH*	(G24)	b. Nov. 23, 1791	d. Mar. 28, 1818
		m.	John Coen*
		b. Dec. 24, 1792	d. Feb. 2, 1871
SARAH	(G8)	b. Feb. 12, 1793	d. Aug. 23, 1873
		m. Jan. 1, 1818	MORDECAI G. BARNES
		(of Richard & Sarah Gilbert)	
		b. Aug. 13, 1791	d. April 30, 1866
MARY		b. Mar. 17, 1794	d. June 16, 1794
JARRETT or JERRARD		b. May 22, 1795	d.
		m.	SARAH BARNES
		(of Ford & Mary Gilbert)	
		b. Jan. 24, 1796	d.
		(Issue, two children)	
Son		b. July 25, 1796	d. Aug. 2, 1796
JOSEPH	(G26)	b. July 18, 1797	d.
		m. 1839	Sarah P. Patterson
		b.	d. 1845
		m. 1846	m. Catherine S. Hone
Son		b. Oct. 20, 1798	d. Oct. 20, 1798
NANCY*	(G24)	b. Dec. 5, 1799	d. June 7, 1866
		m.	John Coen*
		b. Dec. 24, 1792	d. Feb. 2, 1871
AQUILA		b. Mar. 27, 1801	d. Sept. 2, 1801
AMOS	(G27)	b. June 11, 1802	d. Mar. 18, 1889
		m. Dec. 24, 1829	Sarah Bell
		b.	d. Oct. 24, 1860
EVAN	(G28)	b. July 30, 1803	d. July 7, 1875
		m. April 26, 1838	Eliza Ann Taylor
		(of John and Mary Elliott)	
		b. Feb. 28, 1802	d. Oct. 8, 1844
Child		b.	d. in infancy
AQUILA	(G29)	b. Sept. 13, 1806	d. Mar. 9, 1888
		m.	Martha Coen*
		b. Feb. 4, 1804	d. Nov. 25, 1882
		(No issue)	

Issue of THOMAS & SARAH BARNES.
(E-4)

JOHN   (G24) b. Dec. 24, 1792 d.   Feb. 2, 1871
                       m.   ELIZABETH BAILEY
                       b. Nov. 23, 1791 d. Mar. 28, 1818
                       m.   NANCY BAILEY
                       b. Dec. 5, 1799 d. June 7, 1866
                       _____

MARY   b.   d.

_____

Issue of BENEDICT & Mary Morgan.
(E-16)

EZRA   b. Nov. 11, 1803 d.
                       _____

Issue of James & ARABELLA BARNES.
(E-4)

RICHARD	b.	d.
JOHN & JAMES	b.	d.
ELIZABETH	b.	d.
SAMUEL	b.	d.
MORGAN	b.	d.
EVAN	b.	d.
DAVID	b.	d.

WILLIAM   (G33)   b. Mar. 14, 1769   d.   Feb. 9, 1824
                               m.   Mary
                               b.   Mar., 1769   d.   Feb. 7, 1809
                               m.   Mary H. Paullin
                               b. Oct. 15, 1774   d.   May 17, 1853
                               (After death of Husband she
                               m. Aug. 3, 1826   John Katts.

William died at Lower Alloways Creek, Salem Co., New Jersey.
Will dated Jan. 23, 1818 and probated at Salem County, Feb. 19, 1824,
Book 'C' of Wills, pp 133.

Issue of JOHN & —————.
(F-1)

ELLEN   b.   d.
                         m.   William F. Evans.

Issue of AMOS & Ann Catherine —————
(F-2)

WILLIAM FORD §   (H1)   b.   1816   d. Feb. 22, 1886
                         m.   Sarah Eliz. Hollis §
                         b.   1824   d. May 17, 1880

AMOS D. §   b.   d.   1890
(Pvt. 1. R. P. H. B.   Co. G. 13th Md. Inf.
April 8, '65, May 29, '65.)   Civil War. Union Soldier.

GEO. WASHINGTON   (H2)   b.   d.

MARY A. §   b. Sept. 1, 1820   d. Feb. 10, 1871
                         m.   Christian Case
                         b. Mar. 12, 1812   d. Jan. 29, 1889

(The graves of AMOS D. and Mary A. Case may be found in Angel Hill
Cemetery, Havre de Grace, and beside them will be found the graves of
Amos and Ann Catherine (F-2), and it is therefore assumed that Amos D.
and Mary A. are children of Amos and Ann Catherine. Furthermore no
doubt Amos was named for his father, and Mary A(nn)? for her grand-
mother and mother.
We do know that William Ford and Geo. Washington were brothers of
Amos D. and Mary A.)

Issue of BENNETT & —————.
(F-1)

THOMAS BENNETT	b.	d.
ELIZABETH HAUFMAN	b.	d.
WILLIAM HENRY	b.	d.
JOHN ROBERT	b.	d.

Issue of RICHARD & Mary K. Myers.
(F-1)

GEO. WASHINGTON § (H7)	b. Sept. 17, 1812	d.　May 16, 1880
	m.	Sarah Jane Heverin §
		(nee Morgan)
	b. Sept. 16, 1815	d.　Jan. 22, 1857
	m.	Rachel Kirby §
	b. Jan.　26, 1837	d.　Dec. 15, 1893
EMILY M. § (H8)	b. Nov. 16, 1816	d.　Mar. 31, 1885
	m.	Sam'l H. Reasin §
	b. Dec.　2, 1818	d.　July 14, 1872
ARABELLA	b.	d.
	m.	Harry Faulkner
LYDIA	b.	d.
	m.	Alex. Henry
ELIZABETH	b.	d.
	m.	Alex. Barr.

Issue of HENRY & Sarah B. Whitaker.
(F-1)

AMOS PLATT		b. Oct. 19, 1824	d. June 29, 1825

HESTERANN §	(H9)	b. Jan. 4, 1826	d. April 4, 1911
		m. Aug. 1, 1843	John B. Murphy
		m.	B. F. Heath §
		b. Dec. 1, 1812	d. Oct. 5, 1881
		(No issue)	

BENNETT W. §	(H10)	b. Oct. 17, 1827	d. Mar. 13, 1876
		m.	Hannah J. Wills §
		b. Aug. 9, 1836	d. June 3, 1912

JOHN HENRY §		b. June 18, 1830	d. Mar. 13, 1871
		m.	Mary E. Morgan §
		(One child	d. young) §
		m.	Widow Simmons ?

JAMES WILLIAM §	(H11)	b. Oct. 8, 1832	d. Sept. 29, 1900
		m. June 2, 1864	Mary Seneca §
		b. Mar. 2, 1843	d. April 9, 1922

FORD AMOS		b. July 24, 1835	d. Sept. 18, 1837

Issue of HENRY & Eliza Kenly.
(F-1)

SARAH ELIZABETH §	(H12)	b. May 8, 1842	d. April 1, 1897
		m. Jan. 31, 1861	James Hopper §
		b. Dec. 3, 1832	d. June 26, 1902

MARY FRANCES §		b. Jan. 14, 1844	d. July 26, 1848

GEORGE ALFRED §		b. Jan. 19, 1846	d. Aug. 3, 1848

Issue of WILLIAM & Caroline W. Donohoo.
(F-1)

BENNETT W. § (H13)	b. Oct. 15, 1839	d. Dec. 12, 1872
(1st Sgt. 11th Inf. Co. H, Sept. 10, '61, July 7, '65. Veteran Transf. to 2nd Md. Inf. Civil War.)	m. Mar. 28, 1864	Margaret Tigner
	b.	d. Jan. 3, 1882
AMANDA CAROLINE §	b. Mar. 11, 1841	d. July 4, 1927
	(Un-married)	
JOHN SAPPINGTON	b. Feb. 12, 1843	d. May 19, 1926
(Civil War. Pvt. 1 R. P. H. B. Inf. Co. G, Feb. 28, '65, May 29, '65.)	m.	John Alma Allender
	(No issue)	
GEORGIANNA TEXAS	b. April 7, 1846	d. May 10, 1895
	m.	Wm. T. Fields
MARY ANN	b. Sept. 28, 1847	d. Oct. 20, 1920
	(Un-married)	
WILLIAM WOOD	b. Oct. 10, 1849	d. Sept. 22, 1922
	m.	Catherine Myers
	(No issue)	
DANIEL THOMAS §	b. Feb. 23, 1852	d. April 6, 1878
	(Un-married)	

Issue of JOHN & Elizabeth Barnes ?
(F-3)

BENNETT	b.	d.
JOHN ?	b. 1816	d.

(The Will of JOHN BARNES of Amos mentions, Son BENNETT and unborn child.

Inasmuch as this child was born shortly after the father's death it is probable that the mother named it for its father, JOHN.

Furthermore, the records at the Churchville Presbyterian Church show a JOHN BARNES of John as becoming a member, Nov. 23, 1834, he being a young man at the time.)

Issue of MORDECAI GILBERT & SARAH BAILEY.
(F-6; F-9)

ELIZABETH	(H16)	b. Jan. 14, 1819 d. April 25, 1882
		m. Jan. 19, 1837 Thos. C. Fletcher
		b. Sept. 20, 1796 d. Jan. 17, 1847

WINSTON*

b. July 24, 1820   d.   Nov. 6, 1863
m. Jan. 28, 1858   Maria H. Elsey
Widow married McFee, Atty.
Chicago, Ill.

RICHARD III*   (H17)

b. Mar. 27, 1822   d.   Mar. 20, 1893
m. April 18, 1850   MARY JANE BAILEY*
(of Wm. Lloyd & Amelia Holaday)
b.   Oct. 3, 1822   d. July   6, 1901

EDWIN   (H18)

b.   Dec. 4, 1823   d.   Sept. 20, 1882
m. June 23, 1863   Catherine Ruff
b. Sept. 14, 1833   d.   Sept.   5, 1898

ELLEN

b.   May 14, 1826   d. Nov.   7, 1837

SARAH*

b.   Jan. 5, 1832   d. Dec.,   1916
m.   John G. Thompson*
b.   1831   d.   April 5, 1897

Issue; (One Child,   d. in infancy)

JOSEPH ASAEL

b.   Dec. 4, 1836   d. in Phila., Pa.
(Un-married)

Issue of RICHARD Jr. & Susanna Osborn.
(F-6)

SARAH ANN*	(H19)	b. Dec. 6, 1832 d. Aug. 25, 1901
		m. June 14, 1855 Aquila E. Treadway*
		b. Nov. 4, 1826 d. Nov. 9, 1887

RICHARD AMOS*	(H20)	b. Feb. 12, 1834 d. May 21, 1913
		m. Mar. 14, 1861 Mary F. Noble*
		b. Jan. 18, 1829 d. Dec. 17, 1887
		m. Nov. 7, 1894 Mary V. Parker
		(No issue)

MARY*	b. April 16, 1835 d. July 17, 1835

WILLIAM HARRISON*	b. Feb. 26, 1837 d. Aug. 19, 1837

MARY ELIZABETH*	b. Dec. 29, 1838 d. Aug. 31, 1918
	(Un-married)

WILLIAM HENRY*	b. Nov. 3, 1840 d. July 21, 1928
	(Un-married)

FRANCES CORDELIA*	b. July 21, 1843 d. Feb. 21, 1906
	(Un-married)

Issue of FORD & Mary A. Osborn.
(F-7)

ELIZABETH	(H21)	b. Mar. 7, 1823 d. Feb. 16, 1902
		m. Jarrett E. Ward
		b. d. Jan. 31, 1898

Issue of JOHN HAWKINS & Ann Smith.
(F-7)

SUSAN   (H22)   b. Oct. 26, 1833 d. Nov. 23, 1926
                          m. May 5, 1858   Wm. Boyd Herbert
                          b.   d.

MARTHA ANN¶   (H23)   b. July 11, 1840 d. Jan. 28, 1925
                          m.   Wm. Finney Hanna¶
                          b.   1835 d. Mar. 11, 1875

HANORA¶   (H48)   b. Mar. 16, 1844 d.   Nov. 3, 1868
                          m. Mar. 24, 1866 Amos V. Bailey¶
                          (of John & Harriett Barnes)
                          b. Mar. 22, 1840 d. Sept. 20, 1917

Issue of JOHN HAWKINS & Avarilla Fulton.
(F-7)

MARY REBECCA¶   (H24)   b. Jan. 28, 1848 d. Mar. 25, 1901
                          m. Dec. 19, 1877 Jas. Harvey Ball¶
                          b.   d.

Issue of HOSEA & Sarah Gilbert.
(F-7; G-16)

AVARILLA¶   b. Oct. 12, 1841 d.   Dec. 8, 1904
                                    (Un-married)

SILAS WRIGHT¶   (H25) b. Aug. 26, 1843 d. July 25, 1894
                           m. Oct. 30, 1877 Eliz. B. Virdin
                           b. Feb. 11, 1858 d. Jan. 18, 1914

GULIELMA¶   b. Dec. 29, 1845 d.   Sept. 1, 1915
                                    (Un-married)

SARAH ELIZABETH¶   b. July 12, 1848 d.   Mar. 9, 1925
                                    (Un-married)

JOHN LUMSDEN¶   b. April 21, 1850 d. April 19, 1878
                                    m.   1874 G. Oleita Bowman¶
                                    b. Sept. 22, 1854 d. Oct. 27, 1913
                                    (No issue)

WINFIELD SCOTT¶   (H26) b. May 16. 1852 d.   Feb. 28, 1891
                           m.   1876 EMMA L. BAILEY¶
                           (of Charles & Deborah Pinkney)

GEORGE GILBERT¶   (H27) b.   Oct. 6, 1854 d. Mar. 15, 1935
(Rev.)   m.   1883 Margt. M. Officer¶

BENNETT H.   b. June 17, 1857
(Churchville, Md.)   m. July   7, 1898 Arabella Steel
                                    b. Oct. 9, 1850 d. DEC - 4 1939
                                    (No issue)

Issue of JAMES & Mary A. Walter.
(F-7)

MARY		b. Sept. 25, 1838	d. Nov. 16, 1838

LYDIA	(H28)	b. Jan. 29, 1840	d. Oct. 22, 1917
		m. Jan. 24, 1867	John T. Pow
		b. Sept. 14, 1835	d. Sept. 15, 1910

ELIZABETH	(H28)	b. Mar. 22, 1842	d. May 23, 1866
		m. Mar. 25, 1858	John T. Pow
		b. Sept. 14, 1835	d. Sept. 15, 1910

DAVID WALTER	(H29)	b. May 1, 1844	d. Jan. 26, 1916
		m. May 5, 1870	Mary L. Charlton
		b. May 14, 1848	d. Oct. 11, 1896

JOHN BUNYAN	(H30)	b. June 20, 1846	d. Oct. 19, 1904
		m. April 4, 1872	Mary E. Hamilton
		b. Nov. 23, 1852	d. Dec. 11, 1894
		m. June 10, 1896	Adah J. Murray
		b.	d. Feb. 1932

HENRY H.	(H31)	b. June 30, 1848	d. Aug. 1927
		m. June 1876	Mary Trotter
		b. Oct. 17, 1855	d. Sept. 24, 1887
		m. 1896	Mary Witzgall
		b. Sept. 27, 1872	

JAMES A.		b. Mar. 13, 1850	d. Mar. 29, 1850

GEORGE W.	(H32)	b. Feb. 20, 1852	d. Mar. 21, 1931
		m. 1870	Eliz. J. Kirkpatrick
		b. June 8, 1850	d. May 22, 1922

ALAN E.	(H33)	b. Feb. 19, 1854	d. Jan. 1, 1938
		m. 1875	Martha Hulin
		b.	d. 1890

WINFIELD SCOTT		b. April 18, 1856	d. Sept. 16, 1856

Issue of ROBERT AMOS & Avarilla A. Gilbert.
(F-7; G-16)

BYRON		b. May 26, 1847	d. in infancy
HARRIETT ELLEN	(H34)	b. Sept. 5, 1848	d. April 5, 1928
		m. Mar. 25, 1875	John D. Webb
		b. Mar. 22, 1843	d. Mar. 9, 1922
JOHN D.		b. June 23, 1850	d. Feb. 8, 1859
MARTHA SUSAN		b. Oct. 11, 1852	d. Feb. 11, 1859
JAMES WILMER	(H35)	b. Aug. 10, 1854	d. Sept. 1900
		m. Nov. 1876	Olive A. McCorkle
		b.	d.
SARAH ELIZABETH		b. July 19, 1857	d. Feb. 26, 1859
THOMAS R. (Mansfield, O.)	(H36)	b. Mar. 21, 1862 m. Sept. 30, 1885 b. July 24, 1865	Lida Scott
MARY AVARILLA		b. May 28, 1863 (Un-married)	d. Oct. 31, 1934
GEORGE GILBERT (RD 3, Salem, O.)		b. Mar. 30, 1865 (Un-married)	d. July 17, 1939
EMMA ELIZA (RD 4, Salem, O.)	(H37)	b. Dec. 22, 1866 m. 1895 b.	Wm. R. Ovington

Issue of ASAEL & MARY A. BARNES.
(F-8; F-6)

ELIZABETH*		b. Dec. 10, 1808 (Un-married)	d. Feb. 26, 1854
WILLIAM A. §	(H38)	b. Sept. 29, 1816 d. Mar. 3, 1873 m. Mar. 31, 1840 PHOEBE BAILEY § (of Aquila & Martha Evans) b. Dec. 18, 1816 d. Feb. 11, 1897	
JAMES HARVEY*		b. May 10, 1820	d. July 19, 1883
CHARLES LEWIS*		b. Nov. 14, 1824	d. June 2, 1895

Issue of Amos & SARAH BAILEY.
(F-8)

MARY		b. Nov. 4, 1804 d.
BENNETT		b. Feb. 28, 1806 d. m. Martha McComas
AQUILA		b. Oct. 24, 1807 d. Dec. 17, 1893 m. Oct. 2, 1832 Eliza Forrester
SOPHRONIA		b. Jan. 27, 1809 d.
ELIZABETH		b. Feb. 15, 1811 d.
GEORGE		b. July 29, 1814 d.
JAMES		b. d.
AMOS		b. Mar. 1, 1817 d.
SARAH¶	(G12)	b. Jan. 31, 1820 d. Mar. 13, 1903 m. Dec. 15, 1840 HOSEA BARNES¶ (of Gregory & Eliz. Hawkins) b. Aug. 29, 1816 d. May 7, 1900
AVARILLA	(G14)	b. Aug. 24, 1823 d. July 14, 1916 m. May 28, 1846 ROBT. A. BARNES (of Gregory & Elizabeth Hawkins) b. Jan. 19, 1821 d July 12, 1898

Issue of SHADRACH & MARY ANN BARNES.
(F-8; F-7)

FRANCIS AUGUSTUS	b. April 24, 1836	d. June 28, 1855
MARTHA‡	b. June 28, 1839	d. Dec. 8, 1867
HENRY HARRISON‡	b. Feb. 14, 1841	d. April 29, 1908
MARY ELIZABETH (H39)	b. Mar. 26, 1844	d. Mar. 14, 1927
	m. April 28, 1870	Wm. Henry McVey
	b. Jan. 25, 1840	d. Sept. 21, 1918
BENNETT GILBERT	b. Dec. 30, 1847	d. Aug. 19, 1849
AVARILLA JANE (Salem, O.)	b. Oct. 21, 1854	d. July 12, 1939 (Un-married)

Issue of AQUILA & Martha Evans.
(F-8)

EMILY B.	b.	d. 1890
	m.	William Loflin
	b.	d.
MARTHA	b.	d. in childhood.
HARRIET†	b. Jan. 21, 1815	d. Feb. 19, 1851
	m.	Alfred Mitchell
	b.	d.
ELIZABETH	b. 1816	d. 1870
PHOEBE§ (H38)	b. Dec. 18, 1816	d. Feb. 11, 1897
	m. Mar. 31, 1840	Wm. A. BAILEY§
	(of Asael & Mary A. Barnes)	
	b. Sept. 29, 1816	d. Mar. 3, 1873
ASAEL	b. 1818	d. 1839

Issue of JOHN & HARRIETT BARNES.
(F-8; F-7)

ELLEN	(H40)	b. Nov. 16, 1819	d.
		m.	Smith Loflin
GEORGE‡	(H41)	b. Mar. 7, 1821	d. Oct. 25, 1910
		m.	Eliz. Spencer‡
		b. 1827	d. Mar. 10, 1879
		m.	Alice S. Ball‡
		b. Sept. 7, 1839	d. May 12, 1895
MARY‡	(H42)	b. Jan. 5, 1822	d. Mar. 1, 1894
		m.	W. S. Bowman‡
		b. Jan. 17, 1822	d. June 17, 1901
WILLIAM‡	(H43)	b. July 7, 1823	d. Feb. 11, 1905
		m. May 31, 1849	Priscilla Bowman‡
		b. Sept. 12, 1831	d. May 11, 1886
SARAH	(H44)	b. Nov. 9, 1827	d. June 27, 1912
		m. Jan. 13, 1848	John R. Spencer
		b. Aug. 16, 1825	d. Feb. 3, 1908
JOHN BUNYAN‡		b. Sept. 1829	d. Sept. 26, 1886
		(Un-married)	
ELIZABETH	(H45)	b. Nov. 4, 1833	d. Aug. 2, 1915
		m.	David Weikert
		b. 1801	d. 1886
JOSIAH¶	(H46)	b. Sept. 10, 1835	d. Jan. 24, 1920
		m. Feb. 14, 1870	Hannah J. Boyle¶
		b. Mar. 9, 1847	d. Mar. 8, 1918
HARRIETT	(H47)	b. Mar. 21, 1837	d. Jan. 17, 1923
		m.	Robert Dick
		b. Aug. 9, 1831	d. Sept. 22, 1912
AMOS V.¶	(H48)	b. Mar. 22, 1840	d. Sept. 20, 1917
		m. Mar. 24, 1866	HANORA BARNES¶
		(of John Hawkins & Ann Smith)	
		m. Jan. 29, 1873	Mary P. Grey¶
		b. Dec. 29, 1854	d. June 3, 1884
		m. Mar. 29, 1888	Annie E. Galloway¶
			(nee Willey)
		b. Feb. 28, 1852	d. April 10, 1939

Issue of CHARLES & Deborah Pinkney.
(F-8)

HENRIETTA	b. Sept. 3, 1833	d.
	m.	Edwin Frost

WILLIAM HENRY	b. Aug. 17, 1836	d.
	m.	Elizabeth ——

CHARLIE	b. Feb. 5, 1845	d. April 3, 1872
	(Un-married)	

EMMA L.¶ (H26)	b. July 23, 1853	d. May 1932
	m. 1876 WINFIELD S. BARNES¶	
	(of Hosea & Sarah Gilbert)	
	b. May 16, 1852	d. Feb. 28, 1891

Issue of WILLIAM LLOYD & Amelia Holaday.
(F-9)

REBECCA ANN	(H60)	b. Jan.	5, 1815	d. Oct.	25, 1900
		m.		Ezekiel Moulton"	
		b. Mar.	22, 1809	d. Dec.	8, 1869
LOUISA	(H61)	b. Jan.	20, 1817	d. April	18, 1879
		m.		Jno. W. Hoopman	
		b. Dec.	24, 1819	d. June	5, 1897
ELIZABETH		b. Oct.	14, 1818	d. Mar.	20, 1909
		(Un-married)			
LEWIS JOHN Sr.	(H62)	b. July	23, 1820	d. Feb.	15, 1904
		m. June	5, 1849	Rebecca Stillwell	
				Lippincott	
		(of William & Sarah)			
		b. Oct.	31, 1824	d. June	17, 1891
MARY JANE*	(H17)	b. Oct.	3, 1822	d. July	6, 1901
		m. April	18, 1850	RICHARD BARNES III*	
		(of Mordecai & Sarah Bailey)			
		b. Mar.	27, 1822	d. Mar.	20, 1893
HARRIETT LION	(H63)	b. Nov.	27, 1824	d. June	18, 1877
		m.		Joseph Savidge	
		b. Mar.	29, 1829	d.	1898
FRANKLIN LLOYD		b. Mar.	22, 1827	d. Oct.	1, 1828
LLOYD WASHINGTON		b. Jan.	15, 1830	d. Aug.	27, 1830

Issue of WILLIAM LLOYD & Jerusha Harvey.
(F-9)

Son		b. June	10, 1831	d. June	14, 1831
AQUILA EVAN		b. Aug.	21, 1832	d. Feb.	7, 1836
JOSEPH L.	(H64)	b. Aug.	15, 1835	d. Feb.	1, 1904
		m. Nov. 23		Mrs. Margaret Kenny	
		m.		Miss Tierney	
		(No issue)			
AMANDA	(H65)	b. Oct.	15, 1837	d. June	14, 1887
		m.		John Hooven	
EZEKIEL	(H65a)	b. Dec.	17, 1839	d.	1913
		m.		Sarah Harper	
		b.		d.	1917
RACHEL A.	(H66)	b. Jan.	17, 1842	d. Sept.	29, 1923
		m. Oct.	12, 1864	Jos. A. Patton	
		b. Dec.	2, 1842	d. April	14, 1918
HIRAM L.		b. Nov.	4, 1844	d.	
		m.			
RUFUS BICKNEL	(H67)	b. Oct.	15, 1847	d. Mar.	9, 1913
		m.	1876	Rebecca McGovern	
		b.		d.	
MALINDA G.		b. Sept.	6, 1849	d. Aug.	1936
		(Un-married)			

Issue of John & ELIZABETH BAILEY.
(F-10; F-9)

ELIZABETH   (H68)   b. Mar. 17, 1818 d. Oct. 16, 1908
                           m.   1840 Parker Gilbert

Issue of John & NANCY BAILEY.
(F-10; F-9)

SARAH ANN*   b. Sept. 9, 1826 d.   July 16, 1877

PHOEBE   b. Mar. 28, 1828 d. Mar. 12, 1834

DANIEL STEPHEN   (H69)   b. Dec. 29, 1830 d. April 23, 1921
                           m. July 11, 1864 Susanna Elizabeth
                                              Mitchell

HENRY C.*   b. Nov. 12, 1831 d. Dec. 28, 1869
                           m. Mar. 3, 1863 Mary J. Ewing

MARY JANE**   b. Mar. 28, 1835 d. Mar. 27, 1914
                           (Un-married)

MARTHA RACHEL   b. Sept. 13, 1837 d. Jan.   5, 1900
                           m. April 26, 1870 Edwin Ewing

Issue of JOSEPH & Sarah Perry Patterson.
(F-9)

JOSEPH WARREN		b.	1840	d. Oct. 26, 1858

SARAH ELECIA	(H72)	b. Jan. 10, 1843	d. Sept. 1, 1924
		m. Dec. 24, 1862	Abram Stever
		b.	1838 d. 1881

BENJAMIN FRANKLIN	b. Sept. 24, 1845	d. Aug. 23, 1846

Issue of JOSEPH & Mary Catherine S. Hone.
(F-9)

LUCELIA	(H73)	b. Dec. 5, 1847	
(1840 San Pedro Ave., Berkeley, Cal.)		m. 1869	Hiram Sears Bell

CYLECIA	b.	d.

ELIZABETH ALMIRA	(H74)	b. Jan. 24, 1850	d. Nov. 4, 1935
		m. Nov. 4, 1873	William H. Farrar
		b. Jan. 4, 1841	d. Dec. 24, 1926

VIRGINIA A.	(H75)	b. Jan. 11, 1853	d. Aug. 28, 1928
		m. Mar. 30, 1876	Darius B. Mason

HERMANN A.	b. Oct. 16, 1856	d. June 23, 1858

Issue of AMOS & Sarah Bell.
(F-9)

MARIA EDGEWORTH		b. April 11, 1831 d. May 12, 1853
HARRIETT FRISBEE		b. Feb. 23, 1833 d. Feb. 7, 1921
TWIN BROTHERS		b. April 22, 1836 d. May 1, 1836 d. May 18, 1836
LEONETTE		b. April 9, 1837 d. Aug. 28, 1837
JEFFERSON AMES	(H76)	b. Mar. 9, 1839 d. June 10, 1925 m. Nov. 9, 1872 Elizabeth Brigham m. Mar. 28, 1876 Elecia Burroughs
LEONIE JANE		b. Mar. 27, 1841 d. May 26, 1852
ANGELO AMES	(H77)	b. June 25, 1844 d. July 1907 m. Mar. 23, 1871 Lottie Tibbetts b. Feb. 26, 1855
ROBERT OWEN		b. Feb. 2, 1849 d. Mar. 7, 1870
JULIUS RAPHAEL	(H78)	b. Feb. 15, 1851 m. May 15, 1873 Janet R. Cutter
JOHN HOWARD	(H79)	b. Aug. 20, 1854 d. Oct. 12, 1930 m. Aug. 19, 1880 Margaret E. Jones (of Edmund & Annie)
PERCY S.		b. Nov. 28, 1856 d. May 22, 1858

Issue of EVAN & Ann Taylor.
(F-9)

JOHN T.   b. May 26, 1839 d.   July 19, 1889
                                 (Un-married)

LEWIS LAMBORN   (H80) b. June 21, 1842 d.   Jan. 1, 1918
                                 m. Sept. 2, 1872 Ella H. Huber
                                 b. Mar. 23, 1853 d. Feb. 26, 1929

Adopted by AQUILA & Martha Coen.
(F-9)

ELIZABETH TWEEDALE   b. Feb. 1, 1848 d.   Nov. 2, 1918
                  (H81)   m.   1868 James H. Snow
                           b.   1842 d.   1929

Issue of WILLIAM & Mary ————.
(F-20)

LEWIS	(H90)	b. Oct. 5, 1792	d. April 28, 1861
		m. Nov. 6, 1816	Frances L. Ware
		b. April 3, 1799	d. Mar. 7, 1830

REBECCA	b.	d.
	m.	George Davis

Issue of WILLIAM & Mary H. Paullin.
(F-20)

WILLIAM H.	b. Sept. 16, 1813	d. Dec. 26, 1825

WALTER FRANKLIN (H91)   b. Oct. 10, 1817   d. Jan. 28, 1890
m. Aug. 10, 1842   Mary Ann Thomas
(of Elias & Rebecca)
b. Dec. 19, 1818   d. July 25, 1885

Issue of WILLIAM FORD & Sarah E. Hollis.
(G-2)

KATHRYN ARLENE	(I-1)	b.	d.
		m.	Alex. Adolphus Fletcher

LANDONIA §		b.	d. April　　1932
		m.	John Kenly §
		(No issue)	

SARAH MITCHELL	(I-1a)	b.	d. At age of 82.
		m.	Rufus Wells

WILLIAM HOLLIS §	(I-1b)	b. Oct.　5, 1855	d. May　24, 1899
(Havre de Grace, Md.)		m. Jan. 20, 1886	Emma Day
		b. Mar. 27, 1857	

SAMUEL T. §	(I-1c)	b. Feb. 20, 1857	d. Jan.　22, 1926
(Havre de Grace, Md.)		m. Nov. 28, 1885	Sadie K. Gilbert
		b. Sept. 21, 1864	

JOHN HENRY §	(I-1d)	b. June 9, 1863	d. Mar. 25, 1933
(Havre de Grace, Md.)		m. Jan. 26, 1898	Ella Cross
		b.　Dec. 9, 1865	

Issue of GEO. WASHINGTON & ————.
(G-2)

GEORGE WASHINGTON §		b.	d.
	(I-3)	m.	Mary C. Dinsmore
		b. May 12, 1855	d.　　　　1931

EDWARD	b.	d.

Issue of GEO. WASHINGTON & Sarah J. Heverin.
(G-4)

PERRY K.	(I-4)	b.	1849	d. 1919
		m.		Isabelle Black

Issue of GEO. WASHINGTON & Rachel Kirby.
(G-4)

MARY GERTRUDE   (I-5)   b.   1860   d.
                                     m.   Jno. Nelson Black

GEO. WASHINGTON§   b. July 21, 1862   d. Jan.   30, 1915
                                     (Un-married)

ROBERT LEE   (I-6)   b. July 15, 1864   d. Oct.   23, 1936
                                     m. Aug. 11, 1903   Sarah Malcolm
                                     b. Oct. 21, 1874

RICHARD KIRBY   (I-7)   b. Dec. 3, 1865   d. April   1934
                                     m.   Ann Cooling
                                     b.   1867   d.   1920

ELIZA ARABELLA   b. Nov. 16, 1867
(Charlestown, Md.)   (Un-married)

HENRY REASIN   (I-8)   b.   1870   d.   1926
                                     m.   Theresa Black
                                     b.   d.

EMILY ELIZABETH   b. Nov. 5, 1871   ꞓⴰR 3 0 1943
(Charlestown, Md.)   m. April 7, 1915   W. Scott Jackson
                                     b. Aug. 31, 1852   d. Jan.   6, 1929
                                     (No issue)

FREDK. MORRISON§   b.   d. in 3 mos.

EDITH RACHEL   b. Aug. 2, 1876
(Charlestown, Md.)   (Un-married)

Issue of Samuel H. & EMILY BARNES.
(G-4)

GEORGE W. §		b. April 29, 1843	d. Sept. 24, 1878
		m.	Laura A. Fletcher §
		b. Nov. 8, 1848	d. May 20, 1878
WILLIAM J. §	(I-9)	b. April 18, 1844	d. Sept. 15, 1899
		m.	Esther A. Russell §
		b. Jan. 22, 1846	d. Jan. 31, 1920
MARY A. §		b. Mar. 10, 1846	d. June 8, 1914
		m.	James F. Jones §
		b. April 20, 1844	d. July 20, 1898
SAMUEL H. §		b. Aug. 10, 1847	d. July 11, 1848
ALFRED B. §		b. 1848	d. 1917
		m.	Rebecca Townsly §
		b.	d.
LYDIA		b.	d.
		m.	Richard Jenkins
		b.	d.
ARMOND D. §		b. Feb. 6, 1853	d. Oct. 18, 1873
FREDERICK W. (Havre de Grace, Md.)		b. April 2, 1859	OCT 18 1940
		m. Sept. 1, 1900	Emma A. Sheridan
		b. Jan. 24, 1864	
		(No issue)	

Issue of John B. & HESTERANN BARNES.
(G-5)

WILLIAM §	b. Aug. 14, 1844 d. May 7, 1913 (Un-married)

LEMUEL W.	b. Feb. 5, 1847 d. m.
Issue;	WALTER W.

SARAH ELIZABETH §	b. Jan. 3, 1849 d. June 20, 1850

JOHN THOMAS (1505 Mt. Royal Avenue, Baltimore, Md.)	b. July 12, 1851 d. Dec. 31, 1924 m. Feb. 20, 1879 Mary Alice Kenly b. June 10, 1855
Issue;	HARRY b. Mar. 7, 1880 d. June 2, 1916 m. May Reuwer
	LULU ALICE b. Mar. 16, 1883 (Un-married)
	ANNIE LEE b. Nov. 28, 1885 m. C. Victor Dennis
	FRANK b. May 17, 1889 m. Lulu High
	ELIZABETH b. July 9, 1892 m. Arthur J. Emory

ANNIE K. §	b. Dec. 17, 1853 d. Aug. 27, 1855

Issue of BENNETT W. & Hannah J. Wills.
(G-5)

J. HARRY §		b. Nov. 14, 1856	d. April 23, 1876

SAMUEL RUSSELL (I-10) (4315 Park Heights Avenue, Baltimore, Md.)		b. July 30, 1858 m. Jan. 26, 1898 b. Feb. 22, 1878	APR 1 2 1940 Katharyn Hays

ELMER (Baltimore, Md.)	b. Aug. 16, 1860 (Un-married)	JUN 1 6 1940

MARY WILLS §	b. Dec. 31, 1862	d. Aug. 27, 1864

MARY WHITAKER (Baltimore, Md.)	b. Aug. 3, 1866 m. Feb. 26, 1896 b. Dec. 3, 1869	Jacob H. Williams d. April 19, 1939
Issue;	ELSIE CATHERINE b. Nov. 28, 1897	d. July 26, 1898

CHARLES	b. April 27, 1868 m. April 22, 1903 b. Feb. 20, 1882	Mary C. Lewis d. Feb. 4, 1932
Issue;	KATHRYN ELIZABETH b. Sept. 7, 1906	d. June 24, 1916

KATE WILLS (I-11) (1506 Linden Avenue, Baltimore, Md.)		b. April 30, 1872 m. b. 1870	Howard M. Houck § d. July 20, 1929

JOSEPH	b.	d.

Issue of JAMES WILLIAM & Mary Seneca.
(G-5)

JOHN H.		b. Mar. 31, 1865	d. Aug. 15, 1865

LILLIA	(I-12)	b. Sept. 15, 1865	
		m. Dec. 23, 1891	Jno. L. Morrison
		b.	d.

STEPHEN CLIFFORD §		b. July 26, 1869	d. Oct. 17, 1901
		(Un-married)	

Issue of James & SARAH ELIZABETH BARNES.
(G-5)

LILLIA BARNES §		b. Jan. 5, 1862	d. July 17, 1865

ANNA KATE §		b. Aug. 21, 1864	d. July 20, 1865

HENRY BARNES	(I-13)	b. June 27, 1866	
(3330 Dudley Avenue,		m. Jan. 8, 1896	Katherine K.
Baltimore, Md.)			Mathews
		b. May 12, 1866	

WILLIE MARTIN §		b. June 6, 1868	d. April 7, 1871

JOHN THOMAS §		b. Oct. 11, 1870	d. Oct. 21, 1877

HELEN H. §		b. Mar. 16, 1874	d. Oct. 25, 1877

MABEL LESLIE	(I-14)	b. Jan. 8, 1883	
(Aberdeen, Md.)		m. Dec. 6, 1905	F. H. Morgan, Jr. §
		b. Dec. 17, 1881	d. Sept. 24, 1917

Issue of BENNETT & Margaret Tigner.
(G-6)

LEILA
(Havre de Grace, Md.)
     b.   Dec. 4, 1867
     (Un-married)

GRACE
     b. Jan. 21, 1871 d. Sept. 5, 1872

LOTTIE CAROLINE
(Baltimore, Md.)
     b. Sept. 18, 1872

Issue of Thomas C. & ELIZABETH BARNES.
(G-8)

SARAH ANN
     b. Mar. 12, 1838 d. Nov.   1910
     m. June 29, 1881 Jacob B. Webster
     b. Nov.   1840 d. Dec. 27, 1899
     (No issue)

MARY ELLEN   (I-15)
     b. Aug. 21, 1839 d. Jan.   17, 1929
     m. Jan. 11, 1871 Henry Z. Silver
     b. July 15, 1840 d. Oct.   3, 1910

HENRY CLAY
     b. July 9, 1842 d. Nov. 2, 1872
     (Un-married)

FRANCES ALMIRA   (I-16)
     b. Mar. 13, 1844 d. Feb.   9, 1932
     m. Dec. 23, 1879 Henry A. Osborn
     b. July 18, 1841 d. Aug.   2, 1925

Issue of RICHARD III & MARY JANE BAILEY.
(G-8; G-23)

FRANK MARION §	(I-17)	b. June 12, 1851 d. July 7, 1927 m. May 26, 1881 Jane D. Maires § (of Walter F. & Mary Ann Thomas) b. June 22, 1852 d. Sept. 11, 1918
LAURA		b. Jan. 31, 1853 d. Mar. 16, 1853
MARY EMMA**		b. May 7, 1855 d. Sept. 11, 1887 (Un-married)
RICHARD HOWARD	(I-18)	b. Oct. 22, 1857 d. April 12, 1934 m. Jan. 6, 1898 CARRIE PATTON (of Jos. A. & Rachel A. Bailey) b. May 28, 1870 d. July 25, 1936
ESTELLE HOLADAY**		b. Jan. 18, 1863 d. Aug. 22, 1887 (Un-married)

Issue of EDWIN & Catherine Ruff.
(G-8)

LILLIAN IDA (Ardmore, Pa.)	(I-19)	b. Jan. 2, 1865 m. Jan. 19, 1895 Charles G. Rapp b. Nov. 20, 1860 d. Feb. 6, 1914
ALBERT LEWIS (Edgewater Park, N. J.)	(I-20)	b. Nov. 7, 1866 m. June 11, 1895 Annie R. King b. Mar. 28, 1872
KATE EMMA		b. Dec. 18, 1868 d. Aug. 1869
ELLA MAY (5133 Walton Avenue, Philadelphia, Pa.)		b. Jan. 16, 1870 DEC 2 4 1940 (Un-married)
ANNA LOUISE (5133 Walton Avenue, Philadelphia, Pa.)		b. July 18, 1873 (Un-married) SEP 1 5 1940

Issue of Aquila E. & SARAH ANN BARNES.
(G-9)

ELLEN B.* b. Mar. 16, 1860 d. Oct. 3, 1906

CLAYTON SEWARD** b. April 9, 1862 d. Feb. 7, 1865

Issue of RICHARD AMOS* & Mary F. Noble.
(G-9)

WILMER LEWIS (I-21) b. April 4, 1862
(Belair, Md.) m. June 7, 1894 Ellen R. Chesney
  b. Aug. 21, 1875
  (of James R. & Sarah R. Thompson)

CHARLES F. (I-22) b. June 27, 1865 JUL 1 1 1942
(Relay, Md.) m. Nov. 14, 1907 Amelia Pinkney
  Eason
  b. April 28, 1884
  (of Sam'l Addison & Anna Virginia
  Price)

CLIFFORD C. (I-23) b. May 19, 1868
(Relay, Md.) m. Aug. 28, 1902 Hannah E. Hughes
  b. Aug. 26, 1876 d. Mar. 19, 1919

Issue of Jarrett E. & ELIZABETH BARNES.
(G-10)

MARY ANN	b. July 29, 1841 d. m. Michael Anderson
JOSEPH EDWARD	b. Dec. 10, 1842 d. m. Mary E. Thompson
CAROLINE	b. May 15, 1844 d. m. Joseph McCommons
EMMA	b. Sept. 5, 1846 d. April 19, 1912 (Un-married)
HARRIETT ANN	b. Nov. 27, 1848 d. (Un-married)
SARAH ELIZABETH	b. Oct. 21, 1850 d. m. John Carsons
ALICE REBECCA	b. Mar. 27, 1852 d. m. John Thompson
LYDIA LUCINDA	b. Jan. 2, 1854 d. Sept. 28, 1899 (Un-married)
PHOEBE	b. Nov. 4, 1855 m. John Carty b. d. Nov. 24, 1930
MARTHA PRISCILLA	b. Dec. 10, 1856 OCT - 1 1940 (Un-married)
IDA & JOHN**	b. Mar. 24, 1859 d. Ida — Un-married John — Married Margaret Gorrell
JARRETT LEWIS	b. April 24, 1861 d. Feb. 9, 1936 m. Phoebe Gilbert b. d.
ELIZA JANE	b. July 28, 1864 m. Beverly Klyne b.

Issue of William Boyd & SUSAN BARNES.
(G-11)

JOHN BARNES	b. Feb. 3, 1859	d. April 10, 1903
	m. 1883	Ellen Olmstead
WILLIAM MARDEN	b. June 14, 1860	
	m.	Genevieve Avery
MARY OLEITA	b. Mar. 22, 1862	
	m. 1883	John R. Raines
ELIZABETH HANORA	b. Dec. 10, 1863	d. Mar. 7, 1882
FRANK HAMMOND	b. Dec. 19, 1865	
	m. 1890	Mary Blackford
SUSIE FULTON	b. Oct. 22, 1867	
	m. 1893	Dr. Harold L. Seager
GEORGE NELSON (Davis, California)	b. July 10, 1870	
	m. 1895	Lucy Avery
STELLA ANN (Davis, California)	b. May 3, 1872	
	m. 1898	Frank W. Palmer
ELWOOD F. (Pittsburg, California)	b. Oct. 11, 1876	
	m. 1920	Katherine Cleary

Issue of Wm. Finney & MARTHA ANN BARNES.
(G-11)

EDWIN FULTON   b. Jan. 26, 1866   d. Jan.   1929
                               m.   Varina Herbert

JOHN BARNES   b. May 16, 1867   d. May   9, 1916
                               m.   Martha Staniford
                               b. Feb. 1, 1863

WILLIAM FINNEY   b. Oct. 31, 1868   d. May   1915

HENRY NELSON   b. May 26, 1872
(108 Wyndhurst Avenue,   m. Nov. 26, 1896   Alice E. Jeffrey
Baltimore, Md.)

              Issue; ELIZABETH ANN
                      m.   George P. Dix

Issue of James Harvey & MARY R. BARNES.
(G-11)

AVA FULTON   b. May 16, 1879
(Havre de Grace, Md.)   m. Oct.   3, 1901   Alfred A. Colburn
                               b. July   9, 1874

              Issue; EDWARD BALL
                      b. July 20, 1902

                      HERBERT HARLAN
                      b. Mar. 23, 1904

                      RAYMOND
                      b. Jan. 24, 1909

Issue of SILAS WRIGHT & Elizabeth B. Virdin.
(G-12)

JOHN LUMSDEN   (I-24)   b. Mar. 12, 1879
(Crozet, Va.)   m. Dec. 28, 1903   Minnie M. Perry
                       b. Dec. 19, 1881

WARD VIRDIN   (I-25)   b. Aug. 17, 1880   JUN 29 1942
(Madison, Va.)   m. Mar. 14, 1905   Edna Bell
                       b. Feb. 20, 1886

SILAS WRIGHT   b. Mar. 8, 1882   d.   Jan. 15, 1902
                       (Un-married)

WILSON FINNEY   (I-26)   b. Oct. 6, 1885
(Bronxville, N. Y.)   m. April 17, 1912   Betsy Bacon
                       b. Mar. 4, 1885

BENNETT HOSEA   (I-27)   b. Mar. 20, 1888
(Charlottesville, Va.)   m. Oct. 27, 1915   Isabel Robertson
                       b. Nov. 29, 1895

ELIZABETH CAROLINE   b. Sept. 12, 1890
(856 S. George Street,   (I-28)   m. July 24, 1919   Gibson Smith, M.D.
York, Pa.)   b. July 26, 1889

RALPH   (I-29)   b. Feb. 14, 1893
(Port au Prince, Haiti)   m. Mar. 30, 1920   Helen Weaver
                       b. Dec. 10, 1894

Issue of WINFIELD SCOTT & EMMA L. BAILEY.
(G-12; G-21)

| EMMA | b. | d. in infancy |

| EMMA LOUISE | b. | d. in infancy |

| DEBORAH ANN
(5109 Falls Road Terrace,
Baltimore, Md.) | (I-30) | b. May 25, 1881
m. Nov. 20, 1900 Jno. Paul Tingle
b. April 8, 1876 |

| SARAH GILBERT
(605 W. 40th Street,
Baltimore, Md.) | (I-31) | b. Oct. 24, 1883
m. Oct. 18, 1904 Geo. P. Neilson
b. Mar. 15, 1867 |

| WINFIELD SCOTT
(3318 Richmond Avenue,
Baltimore, Md.) | (I-32) | b. Feb. 20, 1886
m. Oct. 25, 1919 Margaret Nelson
b. May 30, 1896 |

Issue of REV. GEORGE G. & Margaret M. Officer.
(G-12)

| HOSEA
(2 Windyedge Road, Glen Arm, Md.) | b. June 15, 1887
(Un-married) |

| MARGARETTA
(2 Windyedge Road, Glen Arm, Md.) | b. Sept. 23, 1888
(Un-married) |

Issue of John T. & ELIZABETH BARNES.
(G-13)

JAMES		b. Sept. 22, 1859 (Un-married)	d. May 15, 1885
GEORGE	(I-33)	b. April 7, 1861 m.	d. June 6, 1886 Elizabeth Webb
ROBERT		b. Dec. 5, 1862 m.	d. Mar. 22, 1935 Mary Klepper
	Issue;	ONE CHILD m.	died. Anna Dietzel
MARY ELIZABETH (Vinita, Okla.)	(I-34)	b. Sept. 11, 1864 m. May 30, 1882 b. April 28, 1861	d. June 11, 1932 James A. Kenreich

Issue of John T. & LYDIA BARNES.
(G-13)

ANNA (Columbus, O.)	(I-35)	b. July 29, 1867 m. June 5, 1889 b. 1857	Delmore Hilles d. 1920
CHARLES (R. D. 4, Salem, O.)	(I-36)	b. May 12, 1869 m. April 2, 1896 b. Feb. 5, 1871	Martha Schnurrenberger d. April 3, 1922
JOHN B. (Columbiana, O.)	(I-37)	b. June 24, 1871 m. m.	Elizabeth Lannon Mayme Lazarus
REBECCA (Denver, Col.)	(I-38)	b. June 17, 1873 m. Sept. 1, 1898 b. 1865	William DePue
WILLIAM		b. July 6, 1875	d. Oct. 4, 1876
MARGARET (3010 44th Place N.W., Washington, D. C.)	(I-39)	b. Sept. 10, 1877 m. Sept. 20, 1899	Hiram K. Green
HELEN (Salem, O.)		b. Jan. 20, 1881 m. 1908 b. 1882 (No issue)	Charles Butz
ALEXANDER (Cleveland, O.)		b. Mar. 3, 1884 m. (No issue)	Myrtle Echenrode

MAR - 4 1940

Issue of DAVID WALTER & Mary L. Charlton.
(G-13)

FLORENCE LYDIA   b. Mar. 26, 1871
(Salem, O.)   m. April 30, 1896 Jacob L. Coy
                          b. May 30, 1872 d. Mar. 26, 1935
                          (No issue)

JAMES BERTOLETTE   b. June 2, 1873 d. Sept. 24, 1888

LULU LAURETTA   b. Jan.   6, 1875
                          m. Feb. 18, 1899 William Herdman
                          b.   1871

                 Issue;   HELEN H.
                          b. Feb. 18, 1901
                          m.   1921 Morton J. Walker
                          (No issue)

CHARLES LeROY   b. April 14, 1878
(Salem, O.)   (Un-married)

MAUDE ELIZABETH   b. Aug. 30, 1884
(Washington, D. C.)   m. Sept. 6, 1905 Chester C. Thorpe
                          b. Aug. 16, 1881
                          (No issue)

JOHN CHARLTON   b. June 9, 1888
                          m. June 1, 1910 Myrtle M. Hatch
                          b. Nov. 20, 1892

                 Issue;   JAMES COLLINS
                          b. June 8, 1912
                          m. June 1, 1935 Vera Settergren
                          (No issue)

Issue of JOHN BUNYAN & Mary E. Hamilton.
(G-13)

ADA HAMILTON   b. Feb.   2, 1873
(11532 Bell Avenue,   m. July   20, 1901 Saml. Newman Pond
Chicago, Ill.)

                 Adopted; VIRGINIA MAUDE

EMMA ESTELLA   b. Mar.   5, 1875   d. Sept. 27, 1877

ALICE MAUDE   b. Sept. 5, 1877   d.   Oct. 1, 1912
                            m. June 21, 1902   Roy Orval Smith
                            (No issue)

Issue of JOHN BUNYAN & Adah J. Murray.
(G-13)

MURRAY HAMILTON   b. Mar. 18, 1899
(Alma, Kan.)

Issue of HENRY H. & Mary Trotter.
(G-13)

WALTER JAMES   (I-42)   b. Aug. 21, 1877   d. June   12, 1931
                                  m.   1901   Florence   Kendig
                                  b. Sept. 29, 1874   d. Jan.   9, 1936

FRANK CURTIS   (I-43)   b. Jan.   18, 1879
(745 E. 5th, Salem, O.)   m. May 14, 1904   Clara A. Moore
                                  b. Aug. 24, 1879

Issue of HENRY H. & Mary Witzgall.
(G-13)

MILDRED LUCILE   (I-44)   b. Jan.   19, 1898
                                  m. June   1920   Murray Lesh

EDITH K.   (I-45)   b. Mar. 23, 1903
                                  m. Nov.   8, 1927   C. B. Hartzell
                                  b. Sept. 12, 1903

THEODORE ROOSEVELT   b. May   5, 1905

JAMES NELSON   b. Feb. 16, 1907

CATHERINE MARIE   b. Aug. 15, 1915

Issue of GEORGE W. & Elizabeth J. Kirkpatrick.
(G-13)

ALPHONSO (Harveyville, Kan.)	(I-46)	b. July 24, 1873 m. Feb. 25, 1904 b. Mar. 27, 1876	d. May 13, 1936 Gertrude Ross
FLOYD EMERSON		b. Sept. 10, 1875 m. Nov. 10, 1899 b. Feb. 6, 1875 (No issue)	d. Sept. 29, 1938 Nora Harrelson d. about 1921
MARY LYDIA (1206 Tenn. Street, Lawrence, Kan.)	(I-47)	b. June 25, 1878 m. Oct. 17, 1900 b. Jan. 8, 1877	Albert L. Kiene
AGNES MAUDE (669 S. Union Avenue, Los Angeles, Cal.)	(I-48)	b. Dec. 25, 1888 m. Sept. 2, 1911 b. Nov. 18, 1888	William Dillon

Issue of ALAN E. & Martha Hulin.
(G-13)

DORA		b. 1877	d. 1879
HULIN		b. 1879	d. about 1890
ANNA	(I-49)	b. Dec. 19, 1884 m. June 1907 b. 1884	d. April 17, 1918 Clyde Hendricks
WILLIAM (Youngstown, O.)		b. 1886 m. b. 1890 (No issue)	Nellie Schoffner
RICHARD		b. 1890	d. 1891

Issue of John D. & HARRIETT E. BARNES.
(G-14)

NORMAN EARL   b. Jan. 29, 1876 d. Oct. 11, 1899

ADA MAE   b. Mar. 30, 1878
(Salem, O.)   m. June 16, 1909 George J. Hawkins
                           b.

                Issue; GEORGE WEBB
                        b. Aug. 19, 1911
                        m. May 24, 1936 Josephine Hudson
                        b. Jan.   8, 1915

                        JEAN ELLEN
                        b. July 31, 1915
                        m. Sept. 13, 1932 Wilbert Webber
                        b. Aug. 19, 1912

SUSAN AVARILLA   b. July 11, 1882
(Salem, O.)   (Un-married)

Issue of JAMES WILMER & Olive A. McCorkle.
(G-14)

BLANCHE ELIZABETH
b. Oct. 1, 1877
(I-50)
m. Dec. 25, 1894   Ira A. Baird
(328 W. Broadway, Alliance, O.)
b. Dec. 28, 1869

HYNE W. (I-51)
b. Jan. 17, 1878   d. Mar. 4, 1939
(1345 S. Arch Street, Alliance, O.)
m. April 6, 1897   Grace Hamlin
b. June 28, 1878

HARRY AUSTIN
b. 1880   d. 1885

CHARLES A. (I-52)
b. Mar. 30, 1881
(1011 Parkway Boulevard,
m. Oct. 6, 1902   Winifred Messmore
Alliance, O.)
b.
m. April 19, 1925   Violet Sheridan
b.

LORINDA MAE
b. 1883   d. 1901
m.   Walter Matchett
b.

GEORGE RAYMOND (I-53)
b. April 7, 1885
(Harrisburg Road, Alliance, O.)
m. Feb. 17, 1907   Nellie Tullis
m. Dec. 1, 1919   Ada Logue

JOHN
b. 1892   d. young

GRACE (I-54)
b.   d. 1919
m.   Ross Fox
b.

RALPH (I-55)
b. 1896
(229 W. Market Street,
m. 1916   Helen Boren
Alliance, O.)
b.

Issue of THOMAS R. & Lida Scott.
(G-14)

RUTH   b. Nov. 18, 1886
(Cooks Road, Mansfield, O.)   m. Sept. 30, 1912 Jas. C. Gorman II

                        Issue; JEAN
                                b. Nov. 8, 1916

                                JAMES CARVILLE III
                                b. April 16, 1924

Issue of W. R. & EMMA ELIZA BARNES.
(G-14)

RALPH REED   b. Dec. 7, 1895
                                 m. June 9, 1923 Mary Jane Simpson
                                 b.

                        Issue; NAOMI
                                b. April 19, 1928

GENEVIEVE ANN   b. April 20, 1903
                                 m. June 30, 1928 Robert Dunn

---

Issue of WILLIAM A. & PHOEBE BAILEY.
(G-15; G-18)

MARY E.		b. Nov. 7, 1842 d. about 1859

OLIVER T.§ (I-56) b. Oct. 26, 1844 d.
m. Cornelia Williams §
b. d.

WILLIAM COLEMAN § b. July 17, 1847 d. June 24, 1920
(Un-married)

HELEN § (I-57) b. Dec. 26, 1849 d. Aug. 9, 1920
m. Oct. 1880 Otho Green §
b. Mar. 10, 1847 d. Dec. 26, 1917

CHARLES H. b. April 30, 1852 d. Oct. 22, 1855

HOWARD TUSTON § b. Aug. 5, 1856 d. Feb. 24, 1906
(Un-married)

EMMA K. § b. Nov. 23, 1858 d. Mar. 5, 1873
(Un-married)

Issue of William Henry & MARY ELIZ. BAILEY.
(G-17)

GERTRUDE BAILEY   b. Mar. 7, 1871 d. Jan. 18, 1910
                          m. Dec. 16, 1891 C. Harry James
                          b. Aug. 17, 1865

                Issue; LESLIE LAMAR
                        b. Feb. 11, 1893
                        m. June 17, 1916 Minnie Ross
                        b. Aug. 3, 1889

                        MARY MARGARET
                        b. Aug. 3, 1898 d. Mar. 12, 1927

                        WILLARD WATSON
                        b. April 20, 1903
                        m. Aug. 2, 1930 Marion Chalk
                        b. Aug. 20, 1906

_____

NELSON AUGUSTUS   b. Oct. 21, 1877
(Smith's Chapel,   m. June 8, 1905 Ida May Coale
Aberdeen, Md.)   b. Nov. 23, 1876

                Issue; THELMA COALE
                        b. Oct. 9, 1908

_____

Issue of Smith & ELLEN BAILEY.
(G-19)

ALBERT‡

b.   1847   d.   1915
m.   Fannie Jarivs‡
b.   1852   d.   1881

ELLA

b.   d.

EDGAR

b. June 23, 1851   d. June   1930
m.   Cora Dick
b. Oct. 21, 1860

Issue;   HATTIE JACKSON
b.   Mar. 4, 1886

HARRY C.
b.   Oct. 19, 1888

STEVE W.
b.   Mar. 3, 1894

Issue of GEORGE & Elizabeth Spencer.
(G-19)

FLORENCE	b. Aug. 21, 1852	d. Oct. 18, 1922
	m.	Jno. T. Baldwin
	(No issue)	

JOHN B.	(I-59)	b. Mar. 28, 1854	d. Feb. 17, 1912
		m. 1879	Sarah Spencer
		b. May 16, 1859	d. Sept. 25, 1887
		m.	Minnie C. Carroll

SILAS REESE	(I-60)	b. Feb. 13, 1856	d. Feb. 1, 1916
		m. Dec. 21, 1881	Annie E. Carty
		b. May 10, 1859	

GEORGE W.‡	(I-61)	b. 1858	d. 1914
		m.	Catherine Hedrick
		b. 1862	

ELLMER E.‡	b. Sept. 7, 1861	d. July 25, 1879

HARRIETT	b. Jan. 7, 1863	d. Dec. 29, 1938
(Rock Run, Harford Co., Md.)	m. Dec. 6, 1905	Edward A. Baldwin
	b. Dec. 30, 1857	JAN 2 3 1940
	(No issue)	

Issue of William S. & MARY BAILEY.
(G-19)

J. HENRY   b. Nov. 18, 1846   d.   Aug. 1, 1920
                                  m.   Josephine Gallion
                                  m.   1889   Mary Libinski
                                                           (Kentucky)
                                  b.   1862   d.   1907

_____

GEORGE W.‡   (I-64)   b. Nov. 16, 1848   d.   Aug. 26, 1920
                                  m.   1879   HARRIETT BAILEY
                                  (of William & Pricilla Bowman)
                                  b.   Nov., 1856   d.   Feb. 20, 1882
                                  m. Jan. 27, 1886   Elizabeth Holloway
                                  b.   Jan. 14, 1868

_____

JAMES L.   b.   Jan., 1851   d.   July 17, 1890
                                  m.   Jennie Jewens
                                  b.   Mar., 1851   d.   July 15, 1918

_____

WILLIAM S., Jr.‡   b. Mar. 15, 1853   d.   Dec. 20, 1931
                                  m.   Annie Jewens‡
                                  b. Sept. 28, 1855   d.   July 12, 1920

_____

MARY EMMA   (I-64a)   b. July 10, 1858   SEP 1 1 1940
(Havre de Grace, Md.)   m. April 29, 1881   George L. Mitchell
                                  b. Mar. 21, 1851   d.   Sept. 28, 1922

_____

CHARLES C.   b.   Sept., 1865
                                  m.   Lucy Gorrell
                                  b.   Sept., 1861

_____

Issue of WILLIAM & Priscilla Bowman.
(G-19)

EDWIN WILMER		b. July 13, 1850	d. Sept. 4, 1863

ANGELINE VIRGINIA (I-62)	b. May 2, 1852	d. Mar., 1924
	m. Nov. 26, 1873	James P. Mahan
	(of William & Mary McVey)	
	b.	d. 1898

LAURA JANE (I-63)	b. June 26, 1855	d. Oct. 10, 1921
	m. Nov. 26, 1873	Amos H. Ewing
	(of John & Caroline)	
	b.	d.

HARRIETT PRISCILLA	b. Nov. 26, 1856	d. Feb. 20, 1882
(I-64)	m. 1879	George W. Bowman
	(of William S. & MARY BAILEY)	
	Widower m. Elizabeth Holloway	

THOMAS V. (I-65)	b. Sept. 23, 1858	d.
	m. May 2, 1882	Sallie Shultz
	(of Edwin & Marie)	
	b.	d. Sept. 28, 1937

JOHN BARNES (I-66)	b. Mar. 28, 1860	d. July 13, 1933
	m. Oct. 11, 1881	Mary Tollinger
	m.	Catherine O. Beale

RACHEL ELIZABETH (I-67)	b. Feb. 15, 1862	d. Dec. 10, 1938
	m. Oct. 5, 1899	John Runan
	(of John & Annie)	OCT 3 1 1940

WILLIAM AMOS		b. Mar. 11, 1864	d. Nov. 8, 1865
CHARLES HENRY		b. Sept. 9, 1865	d. Oct. 23, 1865
MARY SOPHIA		b. Oct. 18, 1866	d. Sept. 10, 1867

AMANDA OLEITA (I-68)	b. May 31, 1868	d. June 18, 1919
(Jarrettsville, Md.)	m. Nov. 24, 1897	George W. Street
	(of William H. & Sarah)	

WALTER FINNEY (I-69)	b. Sept. 14, 1869	
	m. April 23, 1890	Laura Anderson
	(of Michael & Mary)	
	b.	d. Mar. 26, 1937

ANNIE D. (I-70)	b. June 17, 1872	d. May 30, 1910
	m. Dec. 15, 1897	Henry Kirk
	b.	d. Dec. 21, 1928

Issue of John R. & SARAH BAILEY.
(G-19)

ROBERT E.	b. Nov. 13, 1848	d. June 29, 1888
	m. Dec. 15, 1871	Emma Whitelock
	b.	d. Feb. 16, 1904

JOHN W.	b. Nov. 1, 1851	d. Mar. 8, 1934
	m. Jan. 28, 1880	Roberta Wilkinson
	b. June 21, 1853	d. Mar. 30, 1932

ELIZABETH	b. Mar. 23, 1854	
(Belair, Md.)	m. Mar. 4, 1875	C. W. Proctor
	b. April 1, 1844	d. Dec. 30, 1903

IOLA	b. Mar. 11, 1862	d. Oct. 14, 1890
(R. D., Havre de Grace, Md.)	m. May 11, 1884	Joel Silver
	b. Sept. 18, 1863	

Issue of David & ELIZABETH BAILEY.
(G-19)

| JOHN | b. | 1866 |

Issue of JOSIAH & Hannah Boyle.
(G-19)

M. ADELE
(Cardiff, Md.)

b. July   8, 1872
m. Feb. 10, 1904   Richard Rees
b.

HUGH BOYLE   (I-71)
(R. D., Aberdeen, Md.)

b. July 30, 1873
m. Dec. 24, 1910   Ella Walker
b. May   9, 1873

CARLOTTA BARNES   (I-72)
(1230 Farragut Street,
Pittsburgh, Pa.)

b. Nov. 16, 1884
m. May 23, 1916   Clifford C.
                        Hartman, M.D.
b. Jan.   3, 1887

Issue of Robert & HARRIETT BAILEY.
(G-19)

CORA

b. Oct. 21, 1860   MAR 2 0 1941
m.   Edgar Loflin
b. June 23, 1851   d. June   1930

        Issue;   HATTIE JACKSON
                b.   Mar. 4, 1886

                HARRY C.
                b.   Oct. 19, 1888

                STEVE W.
                b.   Mar. 3, 1894

J. LUMSDEN
(R. D., Aberdeen, Md.)

b. October 1871   JUN 2 8 1941
m. April   1898   May Wells
b.   1868

OELLA

b.
m.   Calvin Amoss
b.

Issue of AMOS V. & HANORA BARNES.
(G-19; G-11)

ELWOOD   (I-74)   b. Sept. 19, 1867
(1812 Riggs Avenue,   m. Sept. 5, 1888   Annie Wakeland
Baltimore, Md.)   b. June 21, 1866

Issue of AMOS V. & Mary P. Grey.
(G-19)

HARRY D.   (I-75)   b. Oct.   7, 1875
(R. D., Aberdeen, Md.)   m.   1902   Mary F. Hawkins

HANORA M.   b. July 28, 1877
(R. D., Aberdeen, Md.)   m. Mar. 11, 1914   Granville C. Boyle
                             b. Feb.   6, 1885
                             (No issue)

OLEITA B.¶   b. Mar. 30, 1881   d. Aug. 22, 1915
                             m.   Rev. Chas. F. Bond¶
                             b. Jan.   1871   d.   1922

Issue of AMOS V. & Annie E. Galloway.
(G-19)

CHARLES VINTON   b. June 24, 1891   d. Dec. 30, 1891

Issue of Ezekiel & REBECCA ANN BAILEY.
(G-23)

CHARLES WESLEY**   b. Aug. 16, 1833 d. Mar. 6, 1872
                         m.   Caroline Wilkinson**
                         b.   1829 d.   1916

Issue; RENNA REBECCA
        b. Sept. 28, 1857
        m.   Daniel Gilbert

        CHARLES LEWIS
        b. June 7, 1860
        m.   Maria Ross Harper

        JAMES COLUMBU
        b. Sept. 27, 1862
        m.   Laura Ruth

        JOSEPH LINWOOD
        b. July 23, 1865
        m.   Clara Haines

        THOMAS OSCAR
        b. Mar. 23, 1867
        m.   Gertie Campbell

        HARRY HILLMAN
        b. April 23, 1869 d. July 11, 1869

AMELIA ELIZABETH   b. Aug. 16, 1833 d. Jan. 8, 1907
                         m.   Jos. Wilkinson

Issue; Son   d. young
        ELIZABETH   m. Joseph Mackin
        GERTRUDE   d. young
        WHINNA
            WILMER   m. Miss Jackson

EZEKIEL COLUMBUS   b. Oct. 24, 1835 d.
                         m.   Amanda Hawkins

Issue; GEORGE ADELBERT
        NORRY
        AFFIE (a girl)

Issue of Jno. Wesley & LOUISA BAILEY.
(G-23)

OSCAR   b.   d.

_____

ANNIE ELIZABETH†   b. Oct. 14, 1848   d. Feb. 17, 1924
                              m.   Wm. F. Reasin†
                              b. Oct. 14, 1847   d. June   7, 1906
                              (No issue)

_____

MARY ADELAIDE   b. Mar. 18, 1850   d. Jan.   2, 1930
                              (Un-married)

_____

HARRY B.   (I-76)   b. June 29, 1852   d.
                              m.   Sadie McGeoch
                              b.   d.

_____

MARCELINE VIRGINIA†   b. Aug.   5, 1854   d. Feb. 26, 1930
                   (I-77)   m. Dec.   5, 1882   Geo. R. Hopkins†
                              b. Nov. 21, 1856   d.   Nov. 1. 1913

_____

REBECCA LOUISE   b. Oct.   3, 1856
(Media, Pa.)   m. Nov. 27, 1895   Jacob Walker
                              b. July 15, 1840   d. Feb. 24, 1934

_____

Issue of LEWIS JOHN, Sr. & Rebecca S. Lippincott.
(G-23)

THEODORE HARBOUR b. Feb. 27, 1850 d. Dec. 17, 1926
(I-78) m. Oct. 16, 1870 Emma L. Cox
b. Dec. 4, 1851 d. Feb. 3, 1925

LEWIS JOHN, Jr. (I-79) b. Aug. 21, 1854 d. Mar. 25, 1927
m. Feb. 26, 1878 Mary B. Leighton
b. April 6, 1858 d. July 25, 1911

SARAH ELIZABETH b. May 9, 1852 d. Sept. 26, 1927
(Un-married)

WILLIAM LLOYD b. d. at birth

REBECCA STILLWELL b. Mar. 15, 1858 d. Oct. 4, 1928
(I-80) m. Jan. 3, 1884 Edw. Wm. Sharp
b. July 7, 1850 d. Sept. 7, 1890
m. July 12, 1904 Dr. Lewis L. Sharp
b. Nov. 11, 1841 d. Jan. 28, 1910

Issue of Joseph & HARRIETT L. BAILEY.
(G-23)

IDA (I-81) b. Mar. 13, 1856
(Philadelphia, Pa.) m. Dec. 13, 1874 George Koons
b. Aug. 12, 1854 d. June 15, 1907

Issue of JOSEPH L. & Margaret Kenny.
(G-23)

LINDA	b.	d.
	m.	Geo. N. Lysight

JERUSHA	b.	d.
	m.	B. H. K. Walker

There were other children, understand died young.
It is not certain that the marriages are correct as arranged above.

Issue of John & AMANDA BAILEY.
(G-23)

JOSEPH L.   b. Sept. 13, 1857   d. April 15, 1858

Issue of EZEKIEL & Sarah Harper.
(G-23)

EDWIN	b.	d.
	m.	

(No issue)

Issue of Joseph A. & RACHEL A. BAILEY.
(G-23)

HIRAM L.

b. Aug. 5, 1865 d. Mar. 26, 1889
m. Oct. 13, 1886 Lillie L. Stiles

JOHN ADELBERT

b. Feb. 28, 1867 d. June 26, 1896
m. Dec. 7, 1887 Anna Regina Doud
b.   d. June 18, 1897

CARRIE   (I-18)

b. May 28, 1870 d. July 25, 1936
m. Jan. 6, 1898 R. HOWARD BARNES
(of Richard III & MARY J. BAILEY)
b. Oct. 22, 1857 d. April 12, 1934

Issue of RUFUS BICKNEL & Rebecca McGovern.
(G-23)

BLANCHE ELIZABETH
(514 N. 53d Street,
Phila., Pa.)

b. Dec. 18, 1887
m. May 7, 1918 Chas. T. Donnelly
b.   d. Jan. 11, 1935

Issue of Parker & ELIZABETH COEN.
(G-24)

PHOEBE

b.   d.
m.   Jarrett L. Ward
b.   d.

Issue of DANIEL S. & Susanna E. Mitchell.
(G-24)

LEWIS LAMBORN

    b. Dec. 2, 1865 d. Dec. 1903
    m. 1900 Lillian Touchtone
    (of Alfred)
    b.

GEORGE WILMER
(Aberdeen, Md.)

    b. Oct. 3, 1867
    m.   Octavia Hughes
    b.

JOHN M.

    b. 1869 d. Nov. 23, 1937
    m. 1902 Carrie Cole

    Issue; EDGAR COLE

HENRY WINTER DAVIS

    b. Sept. 4, 1871 d. young

CHARLES STEPHEN
(R. D., Havre de Grace, Md.)

    b. Oct. 10, 1873
    m. Dec. 26, 1906 Elsie Cole
    b. Dec. 28, 1877

    Issue; RALPH
    b. Sept. 23, 1910

Issue of Abram & SARAH ELECIA BAILEY.
(G-26)

LEONA MAY	b. Aug. 3, 1864	d. Jan. 24, 1880	
	(Un-married)		
JENNIE BAILEY	b. Feb. 20, 1866	d. Dec. 19, 1879	
JOSEPH WARREN	b. Jan. 14, 1868	d. Oct. 7, 1890	
	(Un-married)		
ARTHUR CARLETON	b. Sept. 2, 1869	d. May 7, 1934	
	m. 1894	M. Maude Hawk	
	b. 1874		

    Issue;   LEONA MAY
           b.   1896
           m.   Ralph M. Lott
           b.   d.   1928

CARRIE ADELLA	b. June 26, ——		
(Atchison, Kan.)	(Un-married)		
RAY HOWARD	b. Sept. 1, 1874		
(Effingham, Kan.)	m.	Inez McFarland	
	b.	d. 1928	
	(No issue)		
RALPH ROY	b. Aug. 28, 1876		
(Ely, White Pine Co., Nevada)	m.	Treville Spell	

    Issue;   LLOYD ORR
           m.   Edna ————
           WARREN CLAYTON
           m.   Opal Sturtan
           RALPH VERNE
           m.   Christine ————
           ROBERT ROY
           DOROTHY
           LYLE

ERNEST CLAYTON	b. Sept. 13, 1878	d. 1934	
	m.	Charlotte Henderson	

    Issue;   ROY ESTEL   (14 W. 75 St., N. Y. C.)
           m.   Ev'lyn ————

FRANK ABRAM	b. Jan. 14, 1881		
(Effingham, Kan.)	m.	Daisie McFarland	

    Issue;   CORAL NADINE
           b.   1906
           m.   Owen Allen
           GENEVA FAY
           b.   1908
           m.   Sherman McAmis
           MILDRED LORENE
           b.   1915
           ELEANOR MAXINE
           b.   1922

Issue of Hiram Sears & LUCELIA BAILEY.
(G-26)

CLIFFORD   b. Jan.   1895 d. Jan.   9, 1895

Issue of William H. & ELIZABETH A. BAILEY.
(G-26)

FREDERICK WM.	b. Aug. 22, 1877 (Un-married)
EDNA (7112 High St., Maplewood, Mo.)	b. June 2, 1886 (Un-married)
GLENN	b. Mar. 13, 1889 (Un-married)

Issue of Darius & VIRGINIA A. BAILEY.
(G-26)

LOLIE BELL	b. 1877 d. in infancy
ALBERT LAWRENCE	b. 1880 d. 1885
EDITH VERNE (1840 San Pedro Ave., Berkeley, Cal.)	b. Oct. 25, 1878 m. Sept. 3, 1907 G. B. Cawthorne b.
	Issue; ELIZABETH VERNE b. June 15, 1908 RUTH VIRGINIA b. July 3, 1910
ORA LOTTIE (1844 San Pedro Ave., Berkeley, Cal.)	b. July 15, 1882 m. Dec. 25, 1906 Edward S. Moles b.
	Issue; VIRGINIA ANN b. Sept. 25, 1910 m. Sept. 13, 1934 William Fair ELEANOR JEANETTE b. April 15, 1913

Issue of JEFFERSON AMES & Elizabeth Brigham.
(G-27)

DR. CHAS. WHITNEY (I-85) (Hebron, Ill.)	b. Oct. 20, 1874 m. Nov. 3, 1904 b. Nov. 7, 1874	Ida Groesbeck

Issue of JEFFERSON AMES & Elecia Burroughs.
(G-27)

AMOS WASHINGTON	b. Jan. 7, 1877 m. about 1907 b. m. Oct. 12, 1920 b. Nov. 11, 1876 m. Mar. 14, 1930 b. Oct. 18, (1874?)	Mrs. Emma Jones Minnie Roberts d. about 1924 Mrs. Mary A. Hunter
SARAH ELIZABETH	b. Feb. 15, 1878 m. May 8, 1898 b.	Jos. Elmer Gore
Issue; GLADYS	b. April 2, 1904 m. June 1928	Lloyd R. Farmer
Issue;		JANET ELIZABETH b. Aug. 6, 1937
GERALD McPHERSON	b. Dec. 27, 1879	d. Jan. 6, 1880
WEAVER McPHERSON (Livingston, Cal.) (I-87)	b. Dec. 8, 1880 m. Oct. 23, 1907 b. Mar. 25, 1884	Edna May Gore
AGNES OPHELIA	b. Jan. 4, 1883 m.	Fred W. Hillengas
Issue; WILLIAM GRESHAM	b. May, 1918	
ALICE ELIZABETH	b. Oct. 3, 1922	
AQUILA SANFORD	b. Mar. 1, 1887 m. b. (No issue)	Leah Thomas
THOMAS JEFFERSON	b. Sept. 14, 1888 (Un-married)	

Issue of ANGELO AMES & Lottie Tibbetts.
(G-27)

MABEL RUTH   b. May 10, 1873 d. Sept.   1901

EFFIE LEONIE   b. Feb. 9, 1875
(Berkeley, Cal.)   (Un-married)

PERCY S.   b. April 12, 1879 d. April 15, 1881

IRVING RATTAN   (I-88) ·   b. April 3, 1881
(Brentwood, Cal.)   m. June 16, 1906 Lottie L. Sherman
                                b. Nov. 3, 1880

EDITH CHARLOTTE   b. Aug. 19, 1883
(Box 527, R. F. D.,   (Un-married)
Berkeley, Cal.)

MARK GROVER   b. Sept. 29, 1886
(Berkeley, Cal.)   m.   1915 Alice Adair
                                (No issue)

LLOYD EVAN   (I-89)   b. Jan. 22, 1889
(Alvarado, Cal.)   m. June 20, 1928 Valborg Hansen
                                b. ~~Feb. 2, 1896~~
                                ~~Jan 3 1897~~

HARRIETT ANGELE   b. Mar. 24, 1894
(Soquel, Cal.)   (Un-married)

Issue of JULIUS R. & Janet R. Cutter.
(G-27)

LEWIS HOMER   b. Feb. 24, 1874 d. May 15, 1877

FORREST CUTTER   (I-91)   b. July 13, 1880 d. Mar.   1934?
(San Francisco, Cal.)   m. June   1903 Mary Farrell
                                b. Aug. 26, 1881

Issue of JOHN HOWARD & Margaret ———.
(G-27)

GUY HOWARD | b. July 4, 1883 d. Mar. 1914
m. Vivian Duke
(No issue)

ANNIE BELL | b. Oct. 1, 1884
(c/o Dominican College, | (Un-married)
San Rafael, Cal.)

MARGERY | b. May 12, 1891
(c/o Stanford University, | (Un-married)
Palo Alto, Cal.)

Issue of LEWIS L. & Ella H. Huber.
(G-28)

EDWARD HUBER | b. Dec. 18, 1874
(6532 Cedar Avenue, | m. June 6, 1910 Elma M. Caffrey
Merchantsville, N. J.) | b.

Issue; CATHERINE HUBER
b. Mar. 19, 1911

ROBERTA ORR | b. May 27, 1878
(625 S. 48th Street, | m. April 24, 1907 S. Herbert Lund
Phila., Pa.) | b. Sept. 4, 1872 d. Aug. 24, 1936

Issue; OLIVER LEWIS
b. Mar. 12, 1913 d. July 20, 1937
(Un-married)

LUELLA
b. April 29, 1916

Issue of James H. & ELIZABETH T. BAILEY.
(G-29)

HENRY BAILEY	b. Aug. 29, 1870 d. Nov. 2, 1896

SUSIE (Brentwood, Md.)	b. Mar. 11, 1873 m. Dec. 18, 1901 Orville L. Ganbin b. Sept. 28, 1870 d. Oct. 17, 1928

Issue; NORMA　　　　　　(Brentwood, Md.)
b. Aug.　1, 1902
(Un-married)

ORVILLE L.　　　　　(Brentwood, Md.)
b. Jan.　2, 1904
m. April　5, 1927　Jennie Rodgers

MARY LILLIAN　　(Silver Spring, Md.)
b. Dec. 19, 1905
m. April　5, 1927　Jos. H. Prinz

MARTHA
WILLOLA　　　　(Wash., D. C.)
b. Jan.　11, 1911
m. Mar.　5, 1930　Elmer Lambath
m. Oct.　3, 1936　Phillip Ball

LEONARD
LINCOLN　　　　(Brentwood, Md.)
b. Jan.　16, 1913
m. Jan.　10, 1936　Edna Carrick

MARTHA ELIZABETH (Havre de Grace, Md.)	b. Aug. 10, 1883 m. Feb. 28, 1911 Harry Sentmann b. Dec. 12, 1886 d. Dec. 13, 1935

Issue; HENRY
b. Oct. 23, 1912
m. Oct. 24, 1935　Mary K. Heron

Issue of LEWIS & Frances L. Ware.
(G-33)

THOMAS WARE   (I-120)   b. Oct. 21, 1821   d. Jan. 16, 1901
                             m. Jan. 14, 1857   Annie Eliz. Evans
                             (of Samuel & Mary Anderson)
                             b. June 24, 1824   d. Oct. 22, 1864

AMANDA   b.   d.
                            m.   ——— Lumis

MARY   b.   d.
                            m.   ——— Forrest

LEWIS   b.   d.

FRANCES L.   b. Dec. 31, 1830   d. Oct. 9, 1912
                            m. June 12, 1856   Jno. F. Bignell
                            b.   1820   d. April 16, 1874

EDWIN A.   (I-121)   b.   1834   d. April 17, 1896
                            m.   Emma Wilson
                            b.   d.

Issue of WALTER FRANKLIN & Mary A. Thomas.
(G-33)

GEORGE D.   b. Jan. 14, 1845   d. July 10, 1887
                            (Un-married)

JEANNETTE B.   b. Sept. 16, 1847   SEP 2 4 1940
(Havre de Grace, Md.)

ANNA ELIZA   b. Dec. 10, 1849   d. July   1, 1852

JANE DUNN §   (I-17)   b. June 26, 1852   d. Sept. 11, 1918
                            m. May 26, 1881   FRANK M. BARNES §
                            (of Richard III & MARY J. BAILEY)
                            b. June 12, 1851   d. July   7, 1927

Issue of Alex. Adolphus & KATHRYN A. BARNES.
(H-1)

LAWSON LAMAR	b.	d. young
MAY	b. Dec. 25, 1871	d. April 4, 1903
EDWIN	b.	d. young
LANDONIA RENNER	b.	

Issue of Rufus & SARAH BARNES.
(H-1)

MINNIE　　　　　　　b.
　　　　　　　　　　m.　　　　　　Norval Thompson

Issue of WILLIAM HOLLIS & Emma Day.
(H-1)

EDITH　　　　　　　　b. Oct. 12, 1886
(4408 Old York Road,　　m. Dec. 8, 1916　Edw. H. Sherman
Baltimore, Md.)　　　　b. June 5, 1886

　　　　　　　Issue;　SARAH EMMA
　　　　　　　　　　　b. Mar. 3, 1918

　　　　　　　　　　　EDWARD HANSON Jr.
　　　　　　　　　　　b. Jan. 28, 1922

HOLLIS G.§　　　　　b. Oct. 5, 1888　d. Oct. 8, 1895

RAYMOND　　　　　　b. June 6, 1891
(146-01 114th Avenue,　m.　　　　　　Bessie ————
So. Jamaica, N. Y.)

Issue of SAMUEL TREADWELL & Sadie K. Gilbert.
(H-1)

ISABELLE W.	b. Sept.　5, 1886	d. Aug. 14, 1935
	m. June　29, 1918	MURRAY REESE BAILEY
	b. Nov.　4, 1890	

| Issue; | b. Son | d. in infancy |
| | REESE MELVIN b. Aug.　1, 1922 | |

HERBERT AMOS	b. Feb.　2, 1888	
(Aberdeen, Md.)	m. Feb.　26, 1916	Grace Cummings
	b. Sept.　14, 1889	

Issue; HERBERT AMOS, Jr.
b. July　19, 1917

NANCY
b. April 27, 1922

ELIZABETH ANN
b. April　1, 1926

| FLORENCE | b. June　8, 1890 | |
| (Phila., Pa.) | m. | George Kaiss |

Issue; FRANK & GEORGE, Jr.

| CATHERINE | b. Sept. 28, 1897 | |
| (Havre de Grace, Md.) | m. | Wilson Berriker |

Issue; JEAN

| LANDONIA | b.　April 7, 1899 | |
| (Havre de Grace, Md.) | m. | John Stryker |

Issue; DOROTHY D.
b. Dec. 13, 1921

| SAMUEL | b.　Feb. 20, 1902 (Un-married) |

ROBERT	b.　Mar. 5, 1906	
	m.	Gladys Craigg
	(No issue)	

Issue of JOHN HENRY & Ella Cross.
(H-1)

WILLIAM FORD (Linthicum Heights, Md.)	b. May 26, 1899 m. Oct. 10, 1923 Edith Jones b. Oct. 17, 1898
	Issue; JOHN HENRY b. Sept. 3, 1924 WILLIAM FORD, Jr. b. Aug. 21, 1928
LILIAN ELIZABETH (Havre de Grace, Md.)	b. Nov. 6, 1901 (Un-married)

Issue of GEO. WASHINGTON & Mary C. Dinsmore.
(H-2)

Son	b.　　　　　　　d. young
Son	b.　　　　　　　d. young
OLEITA	b.　　　　　　　d. m.　　　　　　　John Sills
GEORGE WASHINGTON	b.　　　　　　　d. Mar. 11, 1933 m.　　　　　　　Mary M. Harmes
	Issue; CARL ROBELING
CARRIE	b. m.　　　　　　　Robert Mason m.　　　　　　　Lewis Votta
ELSIE DINSMORE	b. m.　　　　　　　George Jobes b.　　　　　　　d. (No issue)
DELLA	b. m.　　　　　　　Geo. W. Lowery
JAMES ARTHUR	b. m.　　　　　　　Bessie Parrish
	Issue; BESSIE ARTHUR

Issue of PERRY K. & Isabelle Black.
(H-7)

HARRY H. (Charlestown, Md.)	b. Nov. 21, 1884 m. April 20, 1918 Pauline L. Metzger b. April 3, 1896
EMMA M. (Charlestown, Md.)	b. 1890 m. William Henry

Issue of John Nelson & MARY G. BARNES.
(H-7)

EDITH CATHARINE (R. D., Charlestown, Md.)	b. Aug. 29, 1892
MARY BARNES	b. July 21, 1896 d. Oct. 26, 1935
LILLIAN NELSON (R. D., Charlestown, Md.)	b. Jan. 18, 1898 m. Mar. 12, 1938 John Perkins

---

Issue of ROBERT LEE & Sarah Malcolm.
(H-7)

RACHEL DUDLEY (Charlestown, Md.)	b. Dec. 22, 1903 m. Feb. 20, 1933 Carl Watts
GENEVA PERCY (Charlestown, Md.)	b. May 29, 1906 m. Frank Aguirre m. Worth Gainor
GEO. WASHINGTON (Charlestown, Md.)	b. June 25, 1908 OCT - 8 1941
DONALD STERLING (Charlestown, Md.)	b. Sept. 22, 1916

Issue of RICHARD KIRBY & Anna Cooling.
(H-7)

RICHARD KIRBY	b. April 22, 1900
(Charlestown, Md.)	m. April 27, 1925 Mary Lewis
	b. Sept. 8, 1900

MARGARET C.	b. Jan. 28, 1903
(Cockeysville, Md.)	m. Jan. 28, 1924 Jos. G. Johnson
	b. Mar. 29, 1895

Issue of HENRY REASIN & Theresa Black.
(H-7)

ELIZABETH	b. 1904
(Charlestown, Md.)	m. Edgar McMullan

Issue of WILLIAM J. & Esther Russell.
(H-8)

SAMUEL RUSSELL	b. Oct. 23, 1874 JAN - 3 1942
(Havre de Grace, Md.)	m. Sept. 26, 1900 Norma M. Smith§
	b. Jan. 28, 1881 d. Oct. 19, 1914

Issue; JOHN   (Papeete, Tahiti)
        b. July   30, 1901

ELIZABETH I. T.§	b. June 23, 1877 d. Sept. 17, 1936
	(Un-married)

EMILY BARNES§	b. Mar. 17, 1881 d. Dec. 31, 1937
	(Un-married)

WILLIAM F.§	b. Mar. 29, 1882 d. Dec. 20, 1900

Issue of SAMUEL RUSSELL & Katharyn Hays.
(H-10)

PHILIP HAYS	b. July 20, 1907
(Pittsburgh, Pa.)	m. July 9, 1931 Frances Hearn
	Stevenson

Issue; ANNE SHELLY
b. Dec. 23, 1934

Issue of Howard Miller & KATE W. BARNES.
(H-10)

HALLIDAY BARNES	b. Feb. 10, 1902
(1506 Linden Avenue,	m. April 6, 1935 Alice Lee Kain
Baltimore, Md.)	b. June 21, 1902

Issue of John L. & LILLIA BARNES.
(H-11)

LAURA M.	b. Aug. 2, 1892
(Havre de Grace, Md.)	m. Mar. 25, 1911 Arthur C. Caponic
	b. Dec. 5, 1890

Issue; MARY
ANNIE
MARCELLA
SIDNEY
JEAN
OLIVE

ANNIE K.	b. Mar. 17, 1894
JOHN P.	b. Dec. 31, 1895
WILLIAM S.	b. Dec. 25, 1897 d. Mar. 22, 1937
SIDNEY	b. Nov. 4, 1899 d. Sept. 23, 1910
HARVEY	b. Sept. 26, 1901
	m. June 10, 1930 Catherine A. Fox
CHARLES B.	b. Jan. 11, 1904
MARY F.	b. Jan. 7, 1906
	m. June 24, 1931 Ralph H. Woodward
WALTER F.	b. Feb. 17, 1908
	m. April 30, 1938 Thelma A. Parke

Issue of HENRY BARNES & Katherine K. Mathews.
(H-12)

HELEN MATHEWS (Havre de Grace, Md.)	b.	Oct. 4, 1896	
	m.	Nov. 2, 1918	G. Taylor Lyon
	b.	Nov. 2, 1896	
JAMES GRIFFITH (Comm. Officers' Mess, Naval Air Station, San Diego, Cal.)	b.	Aug. 7, 1899	
	m.	Oct. 1, 1927	Mabel L. Beard
FREDERICK SAPPINGTON (3342 Kenyon Avenue, Baltimore, Md.)	b.	Feb. 7, 1901	
	m.	Oct. 11, 1930	Charlotte Dix

Issue of Frank H. Jr. & MABEL L. HOPPER.
(H-12)

RALPH HOPPER	b.	Aug. 10, 1906	
BLANCHE ELIZABETH	b.	Mar. 11, 1909	
ROBERT LESLIE	b.	Nov. 2, 1910	d. Mar. 31, 1911
CARRIE WORTHINGTON	b.	May 2, 1912	
MERVIN J. ECKELS	b.	June 1, 1915	

Issue of Henry Z. & MARY ELLEN FLETCHER.
(H-16)

HENRY FLETCHER (Goldsboro, Md.)	b.	Oct. 31, 1871
	m.	
	b.	
Issue;	CARLOTTA C. ALTON	
	b.	Feb. 16, 1908

Issue of Henry A. & FRANCES ALMIRA FLETCHER.
(H-16)

INEZ HENRY (R. D., Havre de Grace, Md.)	b. Oct. 17, 1880 (Un-married)
ELIZABETH FLETCHER (R. D., Havre de Grace, Md.)	b. Aug. 2, 1882 (Un-married)
HENRY AMOS, Jr.	b. Oct. 2, 1884 d. Oct. 26, 1918 (Un-married)

Issue of FRANK MARION & Jane D. Maires.
(H-17; H-91)

WALTER DENNY (Baltimore, Md.)	b. May 14, 1882 m. June 12, 1906 Emily Steele Russell (of Samuel Lewis & Julia Boyd) b. Jan. 27, 1880
Issue;	DOROTHY RUSSELL b. May 21, 1909
LILLIAN MAY (Havre de Grace, Md.)	b. Dec. 15, 1889 (Un-married)

Issue of RICHARD HOWARD & CARRIE PATTON.
(H-17; H-66)

RUSSELL WALDO (5151 N. Fairhill Street, Phila., Pa.)	b. Nov. 18, 1898 m. July 27, 1922 Matilda Stefan b. Mar. 10, 1900
Issue;	JEANNETTE b. May 23, 1923
STANLEY PATTON	b. June 26, 1900 d. Oct. 10, 1913
LLOYD HOWARD (Phila., Pa.)	b. June 8, 1902 m. Aug. 23, 1921 Eliz. Strandberg
Issue;	JANICE MAY b. May 26, 1926

Issue of Charles G. & LILLIAN IDA BARNES.
(H-18)

CHARLES BARNES   b.   Jan. 23, 1897
(31 N. Kirklyn Avenue,   m. April 7, 1923   Jeanne F. Hammer
Kirklyn, Upper Darby, Pa.)   b. Aug. 20, 1896

       Issue;   CHARLES GEORGE
       b.   Mar. 2, 1924

       FRANK LAWRENCE
       b. May 17, 1925

       KATHRYN LOUISE
       b. Nov. 22, 1927

Issue of ALBERT LEWIS & Annie R. King.
(H-18)

ALBERT KING   b. Mar. 30, 1898
       m. April 8, 1922   Mary Kathryn
                        Brooke
       b.   Feb. 22, 1896
       (No issue)

RUTH   b. Sept. 30, 1901
(Palmyra, N. J.)   m. June 9, 1923   George Buffington
                        Weigand
       b. Oct. 29, 1897

       Issue;   FRANK BARNES
       b. Sept. 3, 1924

       GEORGE B., Jr.
       b. July 20, 1927

Issue of WILMER LEWIS & Ellen R. Chesney.
(H-20)

RICHARD RANDOLPH*   b. Feb. 25, 1896   d.   Aug. 6, 1896

WILMER NOBLE   b. Aug. 22, 1902
(Belair, Md.)   m. June   1, 1935   Hilda L. Dugger
                     (of Geo. Martin & —————)
                     b.
                     (No issue)

Issue of CHARLES F. & Minnie Eason.
(H-20)

FRANCES EASON   b. Mar. 26, 1909
(1614 Bolton Street,
Baltimore, Md.)

ELIZABETH RAYMOND   b. Feb. 19, 1912
(Baltimore, Md.)

Issue of CLIFFORD C. & Hannah E. Hughes.
(H-20)

WILLIAM COLFAX   b. May   3, 1908

ESTELLE BATEMAN   b. Mar. 15, 1911
(Baltimore, Md.)   m. April 10, 1937   Patrick H. Fetzer

RICHARD AMOS   b. July   25, 1912
(4201 Somerset Place,
Baltimore, Md.)

BEVERLY LEE   b. Mar. 10, 1914

Issue of JOHN LUMSDEN & Minnie M. Perry.
(H-25)

SILAS WRIGHT (Crozet, Va.)	b. Oct. 6, 1904 m. April 30, 1930 Ethel O. Burns b. Feb. 9, 1905

          Issue;   JOHN BRUCE
                  b. Feb. 14, 1932

                  SILAS WRIGHT
                  b. Sept. 2, 1933

HAROLD GILBERT   b. June 30, 1906
(Ivy Depot, Va.)   m. Sept. 2, 1933   Nancy S. Webster

JOHN LUMSDEN   b. Aug. 11, 1908   d.   Jan. 22, 1912

ELIZABETH VIRDIN   b. Sept. 22, 1910

CARL FRANKLIN   b. Aug. 30, 1912
(Box 132, Havre de Grace, Md.)   m.   Ella Simms Clore
                b.   April 8, 1908

          Issue;   CARL FRANKLIN
                  b. June 10, 1935

MARGARET PERRY   b. Aug. 13, 1919
(Windy Moor, Ivy Depot, Va.)

SARAH LEE   b. May 18, 1926   d.   Mar. 2, 1930

Issue of WARD VIRDIN & Edna Bell.
(H-25)

EDNA VIRDIN   b. Dec. 31, 1907
        m. June 26, 1933   John W. Goodall
        b. Aug. 17, 1901

Issue of WILSON FINNEY & Betsy Bacon.
(H-25)

WILSON FINNEY, Jr.   b. May 23, 1920

Issue of BENNETT HOSEA & Isabel Robertson.
(H-25)

BENNETT H.	b. Mar. 14, 1917
LINDSAY ROBERTSON	b. Nov. 4, 1918
ELIZABETH VIRDIN	b. Oct. 13, 1924
CATHERINE GORDON	b. Oct. 13, 1924

Issue of Dr. Gibson & ELIZABETH C. BARNES.
(H-25)

SUSAN (York, Pa.)	b. June 2, 1920
GIBSON (York, Pa.)	b. May 28, 1926
ALLEN J. (York, Pa.)	b. Dec. 18, 1928

Issue of RALPH & Helen Weaver.
(H-25)

RALPH   b. Nov. 22, 1921

Issue of John Paul & DEBORAH ANN BARNES.
(H-26)

LUCILE
(5109 Falls Road Terrace,
Baltimore, Md.)

b. Aug. 23, 1901
m. Oct. 23, 1924   Stephenson Masson
(No issue)

DEBORAH ANN
(2905 Guilford Avenue,
Baltimore, Md.)

b. April 20, 1904
m. Sept. 9, 1922   Lawrence S. Gwyn

Issue;   LAWRENCE TINGLE
b. May 12, 1923

WILLIAM BRENT
b. Oct. 10, 1927

EMMA LOUISE
(6 Orkney Court,
Baltimore, Md.)

b. April 20, 1904
m. Sept. 10, 1923   Chas P. Coady, Jr.

Issue;   CHARLES P. III
b. June 8, 1924

JOHN TINGLE
b. Sept. 6, 1925

DEBORAH ANN
b. Jan. 22, 1926

Issue of George P. & SARAH GILBERT BARNES.
(H-26)

DOROTHY BARNES   b. Aug. 19, 1905
(Baltimore, Md.)   m. Aug. 16, 1929   Chas. B. Hines
                          b. July   7, 1905

          Issue; DOROTHY LOUISE
                  b.   Dec. 8, 1930

                  NANCY CARROLL
                  b. June 24, 1934

SARAH GILBERT   b. Jan.   24, 1908
(317 Taplow Road,   m. June 18, 1932   John N. Curlett
Baltimore, Md.)   b. Nov. 28, 1905

          Issue; SARAH LOUISE
                  b. Sept. 24, 1933

                  JOHN NEWTON, Jr.
                  b. July 16, 1935

GEORGE PEABODY, Jr.   b. Dec. 28, 1919
(Baltimore, Md.)

Issue of WINFIELD SCOTT & Margaret Nelson.
(H-26)

MARGARET   b. Sept. 18, 1922
(Baltimore, Md.)

Issue of GEORGE W. & Elizabeth Webb.
(H-28)

CLARENCE   b.

GEORGE   b.

Issue of James & MARY POW.
(H-28)

JOHN R.   b. Aug. 11, 1884
(Vinita, Okla.)   m. Oct. 20, 1911   Edna P. Sleight
                                 b. Sept. 24, 1892

          Issue;   HARRY J.
                   b. July   3, 1912

                   ROBERT LEE
                   b. Dec.   6, 1919

───

JAMES LEET   b. Aug. 14, 1886
(Vinita, Okla.)   m. Dec. 4, 1909   Golda V.
                                                    Daugherty
                                 b. June 11, 1889

          Issue;   JOHN D.
                   b. Sept. 2, 1912

                   CORA VIRGINIA
                   b. June   4, 1916

───

HELEN JANE   b. Oct. 14, 1897
(205 Delaware St.,   m. May 19, 1918   Wm. Lee Johnson
Vinita, Okla.)   b. Sept. 24, 1897
                                 (No issue)

───

Issue of Delmore & ANNA POW.
(H-28)

LUCILE H.   b. June 30, 1891
(Columbus, O.)   m. June 24, 1922   Wm. B. Davidson
                                 b. May 17, 1888

          Issue;   WILLIAM Pow
                   b. Sept. 4, 1924

───

Issue of CHARLES & Martha Schnurrenberger.
(H-28)

MARY LYDIA　　　　　　　b. Feb. 22, 1897
(114 Chicago Avenue,　　　 m. April 4, 1927　Edward Mason
Youngstown, O.)　　　　　　　　　　　　 Hartman
　　　　　　　　　　　　　 b.

　　　　　　　Issue;　MARTHA MARY
　　　　　　　　　　　b.　May 9, 1928　d.　May 9, 1928

　　　　　　　　　　　MARGARET ANN
　　　　　　　　　　　b. April 18, 1930

　　　　　　　　　　　RUTH ELIZABETH
　　　　　　　　　　　b.　April 7, 1935

GEORGE　　　　　　　　　b.　May 27, 1903
(Salem, O.)　　　　　　　　(Un-married)

HERSCHEL　　　　　　　　b. Oct. 31, 1898
(R. D., Hubbard, O.)　　　　m. Oct. 19, 1928　Katherine Spellman
　　　　　　　　　　　　　 b. April 19, 1886　d.　Feb. 12, 1939
　　　　　　　　　　　　　 (No issue)

WARREN　　　　　　　　　b. Sept. 23, 1904
(Salem, O.)　　　　　　　　m. Nov. 22, 1933　Hazel Greenamyer
　　　　　　　　　　　　　 b. May 28, 1907

　　　　　　　Issue;　RICHARD MARDEN
　　　　　　　　　　　b.　Feb. 7, 1937

Issue of JOHN & Elizabeth Lannan.
(H-28)

WALTER　　　　　　　　　b.　about 1902　d.　about 1918

Issue of William & REBECCA POW.
(H-28)

JOHN MARSHALL	b. June 8, 1904	
(Denver, Col., or	m.	Margaret Hammond
Salt Lake City, Utah)	b.	

Issue; MARSHA
b.   1932

LELAND	b. Mar. 5, 1907	
(Lake Charles, La.)	m.	Mary Ann Fisher
	b.	
	(No issue)	

MARION	b. Sept. 30, 1909
(Denver, Col.)	(Un-married)

MARY ALICE	b. Mar. 15, 1915
(Denver, Col.)	(Un-married)

Issue of Hiram & MARGARET POW.
(H-28)

MARDEN POW

b. July   4, 1904 d.   Oct. 4, 1928
m. June 16, 1926 Stella Porter
b. Mar. 16, 1902
(No issue)

FREDERICK H.
(3010 44th Place N.W.,
Washington, D. C.)

b. June 14, 1909
m. Oct. 29, 1938 Evelyn R.
                            Brumbaugh
b. Feb. 20, 1914

Issue of WALTER JAMES & Florence Kendig.
(H·31)

MARY

b. Feb. 10, 1903
m. June 9, 1923 Theodore Cook
b.

Issue; MARY GWENDOLYN
b. Sept. 23, 1924

DOROTHEA FLORENCE
b. July 7, 1926

HAROLD WALTER

b. June 23, 1904
m. Feb. 1928 Marguerite Baldwin
b.

Issue; HAROLD
b. July 15, 1929

RAYMOND KENNETH

b. July 23, 1907

Issue of FRANK CURTIS & Clara A. Moore.
(H·31)

HELEN ETHEL

b. April 14, 1905

EDYTHE MAE

b. Jan. 13, 1907
m. Jan. 12, 1935 Frederick W. Lyons
b.

Issue; FREDERICK W., Jr.
b. Nov. 7, 1935

MELBA ALICE

b. Jan. 14, 1911

JOHN LELAND

b. May 9, 1914
m. May 25, 1935 Eleanor Gilbert
b. Mar. 6, 1913

Issue of WALTER JAMES & Florence Kendig.
(H-31)

MARY   b. Feb. 10, 1903
                               m. June   9, 1923   Theodore Cook
                               b.

                   Issue;   MARY GWENDOLYN
                            b. Sept. 23, 1924

                            DOROTHEA FLORENCE
                            b. July   7, 1926

HAROLD WALTER   b. June 23, 1904
                               m. Feb.   1928   Marguerite Baldwin
                               b.

                   Issue;   HAROLD
                            b. July 15, 1929

RAYMOND KENNETH   b. July 23, 1907

Issue of FRANK CURTIS & Clara A. Moore.
(H-31)

HELEN ETHEL   b. April 14, 1905

EDYTHE MAE   b. Jan. 13, 1907
                               m. Jan. 12, 1935   Frederick W. Lyons
                               b.

                   Issue;   FREDERICK W., Jr.
                            b. Nov. 7, 1935

MELBA ALICE   b. Jan. 14, 1911

JOHN LELAND   b. May   9, 1914
                               m. May 25, 1935   Eleanor Gilbert
                               b. Mar.   6, 1913

Issue of Murray & MILDRED L. BARNES.
(H-31)

EDNA MAY	b.	July 4, 1922		
MARY & MARTHA	b.	1924		
GLADYS	b.	1926	d.	1931
JOSEPH	b.	1927		
WILLIAM	b.	1928	d.	1937
BARBARA JANE	b. Aug.	1936		

Issue of C. B. & EDITH K. BARNES.
(H-31)

BYRON BERNARD	b. May 5, 1929
BARBARA ANN	b. April 19, 1934

Issue of ALPHONSO & Gertrude Ross.
(H-32)

ELIZABETH AGNES   b. Mar. 28, 1906
(Harveyville, Kan.)   m. June 6, 1928   Dale Marrs
          Issue; MYRNA BETH
              b. Mar. 19, 1930

RUTH GERTRUDE   b. Mar. 23, 1908
(Harveyville, Kan.)   m. Aug. 20, 1931   Norval H.
                                 Garinger
          Issue; JO ANN
              b. July 8, 1932
              CAROL LOUISE
              b. Dec. 31, 1935

MAUDE MINERVA   b. Nov. 6, 1909
(S. B. A. Hospital, Topeka, Kan.)   (Un-married)

Issue of Albert L. & MARY L. BARNES.
(H-32)

CLARENCE KIRK   b. Feb. 18, 1908
                          m. Dec. 14, 1937 Evalyn Rickerd
                          b. Oct.   3, 1907

────────────────────────────

MARY ELIZABETH   b. Nov. 29, 1916

──

Issue of William & AGNES M. BARNES.
(H-32)

WILLIAM, Jr.   b. July 30, 1911
(Monterey, Cal.)

──

Issue of Clyde & ANNA BARNES.
(H-33)

OSCAR WILLIAM   b. July   7, 1908 d. May 15, 1935
(Worthington, O.)   m. Jan.   1931 Gertrude E. Potter
                          m. Feb. 23, 1907

                Issue;   WILLIAM HULIN
                         b. Oct. 17, 1932

                         ROBERT CLYDE
                         b. May 14, 1934

────────────────────────────

Issue of Ira A. & BLANCHE E. BARNES.
(H-35)

BERDELLA HELENE
(3136 W. Liberty Avenue,
Dormont, Pa.)

b. Sept. 3, 1899
m. Mar. 20, 1920 Arthur B. Bault
b. May 27, 1893

Issue; CONSTANCE A.
b. Jan. 11, 1923

EVELYN AVARILLA
(214 E. Raymond St.,
Chevy Chase, Md.)

b. Sept. 6, 1907
m. Oct. 20, 1932 Frederick A. Long
b. Sept. 28, 1904

Issue; PHYLLIS BAIRD
b. Jan. 12, 1934

FERNE OLIVE
(1365 S. Seneca Avenue,
Alliance, O.)

b. Mar. 13, 1910
m. Sept. 17, 1934 Alvin A. Curtiss
b. Mar. 14, 1909

Issue of HYNE W. & Grace Hamlin.
(H-35)

LARUE OLIVE
(210 Grand Avenue,
Edgewood, R. I.)

b. Dec. 1896
m. Leonard Taite
m. Vernon Rodgers
     Wixon

Issue; JOHN
b.

HELEN IRENE
(2827 215th Street,
Bayside, N. Y.)

b. Feb. 5, 1900
m. Feb. 21, 1920 Capt. John G.
     Murphy
b. Jan. 28, 1893

Issue; MARJORIE
b. July 18, 1923
PATRICIA ANN & NANCY ELLEN
b. Dec. 15, 1924
JOHN G., Jr.
b. June 15, 1937

HAROLD DARYL
(Edgewater Beach Apartments,
5555 Sheridan Road, Chicago, Ill.)

b.
m. Nancy Shrewsberry
b.

Issue; THOMAS
b.

Issue of CHARLES A. & Winifred Messmore.
(H-35)

VERA   b.
(Alliance, O.)   m.   George Richards
                              b.
                    Issue; GEORGE, Jr.
                              b.

DORIS   b.
(Cleveland, O.)   m.   John Spilker
                    Issue; WINIFRED

Issue of GEORGE RAYMOND & Nellie Tullis.
(H-35)

MARY   b. Aug. 17, 1909
(Alliance, O.)   m. Nov. 27, 1929 Walter Hoover
                              b. Aug. 15, 1907
                    Issue; NORMA JEAN
                              b. Sept. 20, 1932

GRACE   b. Mar. 11, 1911
(Alliance, O.)   m. April 25, 1932 Carl Keller
                              b. Dec. 30, 1911
                    Issue; CAROLYN
                              b. Aug. 2, 1934
                              DONALD
                              b. Sept. 13, 1936

GEORGE   b. Aug. 19, 1914
(Alliance, O.)   m. Nov. 20, 1934 Thelma Hawkins
                              b. April 12, 1915
                    Issue; BETTY LOU
                              b. Jan. 14, 1937

                              WILLIAM RAYMOND
                              b. Sept. 14, 1938

Issue of Ross & GRACE BARNES.

(H-35)

RUTH OLIVE   b.
(305 East Gaskill Street,
Alliance, O.)

Issue of RALPH & Ellen Boren.

(H-35)

WALTER WADE   b. May 15, 1917
(449 W. Columbia Street,
Alliance, O.)

JEAN ELEANOR   b. May 5, 1919
(Alliance, O.)

BETTY JANE   b. Dec. 13, 1927
(Alliance, O.)

Issue of OLIVER T. & Cornelia Williams.
(H-38)

WILLIAM	b.	d.
	(Un-married)	
CARRIE	b.	d.
	m.	John Exline
Issue; PHOEBE		(Wash., D. C.)
	b.	
OLIVER		
	b.	d.

Issue of Otho & HELEN BAILEY.
(H-38)

HELEN
(Havre de Grace, Md.)
b. Sept. 18, 1881
m. Sept. 20, 1898   Charles B. Burns

Issue; CHARLES WILLIAM
b.   July 6, 1900
m.   Oct. 4, 1923   Evelyn Preston

Issue; HELEN VIRGINIA
b. June 20, 1924
WM. PRESTON
b.   Mar. 29, 1926

VERNON M.
b. Aug. 27, 1902

CARROLL E.
b. Feb.   9, 1906
m. Sept. 19, 1935   Gladys Carr

HELEN LOUISE
b. Jan.   22, 1908
m. Mar. 18, 1933   Marshall C. Waller
b. Mar. 18, 1887

JENNIE MAIDEL
b. Mar.   2, 1915
m. Mar.   2, 1933   Wm. C. Campbell

Issue; ANN ROLAND
b. Sept.   1, 1934

ROBERT B.
b. Dec. 12, 1917

Issue of JOHN B. & Sarah Spencer.
(H-41)

HERBERT S.   b. Mar. 17, 1885
(Darlington, Md.)   m. Dec. 10, 1910 Lena Ryan

    Issue; LENA
        b. June 12, 1914
        m. May   4, 1936 Wm. S. Hanna
        b. Feb. 26, 1914

Issue of SILAS R. & Annie E. Carty.
(H-41)

ORMUND PERCY   b. Mar. 14, 1883 d. Mar. 30, 1883

W. ARTHUR   b. Aug. 18, 1884
(2720 Guilford Avenue,   m. Oct. 30, 1912 Anna R. Bryan
Baltimore, Md.)   b. June 3, 1884

    Issue; WILLIAM ARTHUR, Jr.
        b. Nov. 25, 1913

HARRY M.   b. May 24, 1887
(3300 St. Paul Street,   m. Oct. 6, 1916 Augusta L. Fieseler
Baltimore, Md.)   b. Dec. 20, 1888
                   (No issue)

MURRAY REESE   b. Nov. 4, 1890
(3132 Normount Avenue,   m. June 29, 1918 ISABELLE W.
Baltimore, Md.)   BARNES
                b. Sept. 5, 1886 d. Aug. 14, 1935

    Issue; Son,
        b.   d. in infancy

        REESE MELVIN
        b. Aug. 1, 1922

Issue of GEORGE W. & Catherine Hedrick.
(H-41)

ELSIE	b.	
	m.	Rev. Richard N. Edwards

Issue of James P. & ANGELINE V. BAILEY.
(H-43)

CLARA O.   b. Dec. 1, 1882   d. Feb. 21, 1918
                m.   Charlie Morgan

Issue; RAYMOND
        CIRDUS   b. Oct. 21, ——
        ROBIE V.   b. Mar. 7, 1910
        CLARICE   d. young
        (Morgan married again with
        issue of 3 other children.)

JAMES ALLEN   b. June 28, 1880
(Churchville, Md.)   m. Sept. 4, 1904 Grace Street
                (of George & Margaret Ellen Mason)

Issue; ALLEN LEROY   b. April 14, 1905
        STREET BARNES   b. Sept. 30, 1906
        JAMES ALLEN   b. Mar.   31, 1908
        CHARLES EDWIN   b. Aug.   4, 1909
        MARGARET VA.   b. Oct.   21, 1910
        FLORENCE   b. Sept.   6, 1913
        FLOYD E.   b. Mar.   11, 1912
        RUSSELL   b. Mar.   20, 1916
        ALICE ELIZ.   b. Mar.   25, 1919
        ESTHER IRENE   b. Mar.   25, 1919
        MARY ADELIA   b. Mar.   26, 1920
        GRACE LAURA   b. Mar.   16, 1922
        DORIS   b. Oct.   7, 1924
        STANLEY MASON   b. Jan.   13, 1929

ROBIE   b. Dec.   8, 1887
                m. Nov.   1, 1907 J. Austin Knight
                b.

Issue; HAROLD AUSTIN   b. April 12, 1912
        m.   1936 Grace Watson

WILLIAM OLIVER b. Aug.   8, 1891   d. Mar. 18, 1897

Issue of Amos H. & LAURA JANE BAILEY.
(H-43)

ALICE REBECCA	b.	d.	Nov. 9, 1883
FLORA GARFIELD	b.	d.	May 16, 1882
			(in infancy)

9th & 10th Gen.   BOWMAN   I-64

Issue of GEORGE W. & HARRIETT P. BAILEY.
(H-42; H-43)

IRVIN BERLIN   b.   d. Oct. 25, 1883

ANGELINE ROBERTA   b. Jan. 29, 1882
m. Aug. 20, 1910   Amos Whittle

Issue;   AMANDA ELIZABETH
b. May 28, 1911

MYRTLE VIRGINIA
b. Jan. 15, 1913

ALICE ROBERTA
b. Oct. 14, 1921

9th Gen.   MITCHELL   I-64a

Issue of George L. & MARY EMMA BOWMAN.
(H-42)

PEARL SYLVIA   b. Mar. 18, 1882
(Havre de Grace, Md.)   (Un-married)

ROSE ELLA   b. Mar. 30, 1884   d. Aug. 17, 1889

MARY LILLIAN   b. Feb.   6, 1886   d.   May 6, 1926
m. Oct. 24, 1911   Wm. J. Bonnett

HELEN BOWMAN   b. Mar. 23, 1889   d. Aug. 27, 1889

STELLA ELIZABETH   b. Oct.   3, 1891
(Havre de Grace, Md.)   m. June 23, 1914   J. Lawson Gilbert

GEORGE CORTHELL   b. Mar. 21, 1894
(Havre de Grace, Md.)   (Un-married)

Issue of THOMAS V. & Sallie Shultz.
(H-43)

W. SANNER
b. Jan.   11, 1892
m. Jan.   3, 1914   Hattie B. Preston
b. July   24, 1891
Issue;   VINTON E.
b. Nov. 15, 1914
HAROLD M.
b. Sept. 22, 1917
GRACE M.
b. May   1, 1921
LLOYD ALDEN
b. Feb.   3, 1923

Issue of JOHN BARNES & Mary Tollinger.
(H-43)

ROBERT ASAEL   b.   July 18, 1882   d.   Sept. 27, 1893

WILLIAM ALBERT   b.   Oct. 14, 1883   MAY - 9 1940

Issue of John & RACHEL ELIZABETH BAILEY.
(H-43)

LAURA ELIZABETH   b.   May 13, 1900
(R. D. No. 1, Aberdeen, Md.)   m. April 12, 1922   Andrew E. Markline
b.
Issue;   JOHN EDWARD
b.   May 19, 1923

LEWIS RUNAN
b. Aug. 27, 1930

WILLARD RAYMOND   b. Sept. 12, 1902   d.   Aug. 10, 1910

Issue of George W. & AMANDA O. BAILEY.
(H-43)

BESSIE MABEL   b.   April 8, 1900

Issue of WALTER FINNEY & Laura Anderson.
(H-43)

HARRY OSCAR   b. Feb. 27, 1891   MAY 2 3 1940
(Havre de Grace, Md.)   m.   1917   Annie Martin

LYDIA PRISCILLA   b. Sept. 22, 1892
(Delta, Pa.)   m.   H. McAllister

GEORGE MELVIN   b. Sept. 30, 1893
(Belair, Md.)   m. Mar. 1, 1919   T. Priscilla Livezey
       b. Dec.   3, 1896

       Issue;   WILLIAM MELVIN
           b. April 5, 1920

LILLIE   b. Feb.   8, 1895
       m.   William Johnson

FLORENCE REBECCA   b. July   12, 1897
(Belair, Md.)   m. Nov. 24, 1920   Russell Hildt

MARGUERITE M.   b. Dec.   9, 1898
(Bancroft Mills,   m. April 23, 1919   Otho Calder
Wilmington, Del.) .

WILLARD   b. June 12, 1900
(Sharon, Harford Co., Md.)   m.   Ruth Reilly

NORA   b. Aug. 31, 1902
       m.   Burl Osborn
       b.   d.

Issue of Henry & ANNIE BAILEY.
(H-43)

HELEN   b. Mar. 22, 1903
(Fallston, Md.)   m. May 31, 1930   Ernest Breeden
       b.

       Issue;   ERNEST KIRK
           b. Nov. 18, 1931

           ROBERTA HARLAN
           b. Aug.   3, 1934

Issue of HUGH BOYLE & Ella Walker.

(H-46)

HUGH BOYLE, Jr.   b. Dec. 15, 1911
(Aldino, Md.)

JOHN W.   b.   Dec. 7, 1914
(Aldino, Md.)

Issue of Dr. Clifford C. & CARLOTTA B. BAILEY.

(H-46)

JANE AILEEN BAILEY   b. Dec. 13, 1923
(Pittsburgh, Pa.)

Issue of ELWOOD & Annie Wakeland.
(H-48)

JAMES R.	b. May 5, 1889
CALVIN A.	b. Dec. 25, 1890
MAURICE B.	b. July 28, 1893 d. April 6, 1924

Issue of HARRY D. & Mary F. Hawkins.
(H-48)

HELEN H.	b. July 17, 1903

Issue of HARRY B. & Sadie McGeoch.
(H-61)

LOUISA (1809 Poplar Grove Street, Baltimore, Md.)	b. Aug. 26, 1879 (Un-married)
Child	b. 1881 d. young
RAYMOND (Baltimore, Md.)	b. Oct. 7, 1884 (Un-married)
HOWARD	b. June 15, 1886 d. Mar. 15, 1918 (Un-married)

Issue of George R. & MARCELINE V. HOOPMAN.
(H-61)

WELLMORE HOOPMAN (Boston, Mass.)	b. Sept. 23, 1883 m. Feb. 25, 1904 b. Mar. 18, 1879	Eliz. Worthington
Issue;	EDNA b. Mar. 11, 1905 m. Dec. 16, 1933 b. July 21, 1907	(Baltimore, Md.) Talbott D. Moeller

LOUISE (2100 N. Calvert Street, Baltimore, Md.)	b. April 23, 1885 m. Oct. 18, 1906 b. Mar. 3, 1881	Wm. E. Worthington, Jr. d. Oct. 8, 1918
Issue;	VIRGINIA H. b. April 19, 1907 MILDRED L. b. May 26, 1908 EDWIN L. b. Mar. 28, 1911 EDITH E. b. Mar. 10, 1914 EMILY ROBERTA b. Mar. 14, 1917	(Linthicum Hts., Md.) (Media, Pa.) (Baltimore, Md.) (Baltimore, Md.) d. Sept. 30, 1920

ETHEL (Media, Pa.)	b. Sept. 14, 1887 m. July 25, 1908 b. Sept. 12, 1879	Nelson Worthington
Issue;	RAYMOND b. June 29, 1909 MARGARET b. Sept. 24, 1910	(Media, Pa.)

HARRY	b. Sept. 1888	d. in 6 months, 1889

ROBERT MILTON (Baltimore, Md.)	b. May 25, 1889 m. (No issue)	Eliz. F. Stephenson

LEVIN	b. 1890	d. in 9 weeks

Four other children	all died in infancy	

Issue of THEO. HARBOUR & Emma L. Cox.
(H-62)

SUSAN BLANCHE   b. April 20, 1872   d. April 21, 1872

EMMA MAY   b. July   1, 1873
(8602 Fort Hamilton P'way,   m. June 14, 1893   Fredric Möhle
Brooklyn, N. Y.)

                   Issue; FLORENCE
                           b. Aug. 8, 1896

                         FREDRIC BAILEY
                         b. Feb. 23, 1901
                         m. Oct. 16, 1928   Catherine Mitchell

                         (Issue; WM. PENNINGTON
                         b. Oct. 15, 1935)

FLORENCE REBECCA   b. Oct. 11, 1878   d. Mar. 18, 1915

THEO. HARBOUR, Jr.   b. Jan. 24, 1890
(1207 Frederick Road,   m. Nov. 15, 1919   Florence O. Nairne
Catonsville, Md.)   b. Aug. 26, 1896

                   Issue; THEO. HARBOUR, III
                         b. Dec. 18, 1922

                         WILLIAM NAIRNE
                         b. April 30, 1925

JOSEPH LLOYD   b. Jan. 17, 1892
(54 Greenacres Ave.,   m.   Shirley Gleason
Scarsdale, N. Y.)

                   Issue; JOYCE
                         b. Aug. 6, 1921

                         ALICE GLEASON
                         b. April 17, 1923

Issue of LEWIS JOHN, Jr., & Mary B. Leighton.
(H-62)

THEODORE LEIGHTON
(Cuba)

b. Feb. 13, 1880
m. Oct. 15, 1903　Ida Shifer
b.
(No issue)

LEWIS ELBERON
(Chicago, Ill.)

b. Sept. 19, 1881
m. April　　1909　Eliz. B. Croskey
b.

Issue;　ELIZABETH BROWNING
b. Aug. 15, 1912

HOMER HARBOUR

b. May 21, 1884
m. Nov. 19, 1924　Eleanor Carter
b.
(No issue)

REBA LEIGHTON
(Mt. Holly, N. J.)

b. Aug. 28, 1886
m. May　3, 1905　David F. Shull, Jr.

Issue;　FLORENCE LEIGHTON
b. Nov. 30, 1906
m. Aug.　4, 1932　Donald E.
　　　　　　　　　Stettlemyer
b. Oct. 23, 1904

VERA STEWARD
b. April　7, 1908
m. April 21, 1933　John E. Flanagan
b. Feb.　8, 1907

EDITH SHARP
(417 High Street,
Mt. Holly, N. J.)

b.　Oct. 1, 1888
m.　Oct. 1, 1913　Dan'l F. Remer

Issue;　MARY LEIGHTON
b.　Sept. 4, 1922

Issue of Edwin Wm. & REBECCA S. BAILEY.
(H-62)

FLORENCE BROMWELL   b. June 25, 1885 d. Jan. 17, 1890

Issue of George & IDA SAVIDGE.
(H-63)

FLORENCE   b.   Oct. 9, 1876
(5333 Walton Avenue,   m.   Jan. 9, 1895 Howard T. Wunder
Phila., Pa.)   b.   Jan. 6, 1874

    Issue; EDITH HARNED
        b. May 19, 1896 d.   July 8, 1900

GERTRUDE   b. Feb. 21, 1879
(5027 Walton Avenue,   m. Aug. 19, 1901 George D. Mancill
Phila., Pa.)   b. Sept. 25, 1874

    Issue; GEORGE D., Jr.
        b. April 24, 1902
        m. Dec. 14, 1927 Mary B. Whiteside

        ROLAND A.
        b. Aug. 19, 1911

Issue of DR. CHARLES WHITNEY & Ida Groesbeck.
(H-76)

ALICE ELIZABETH   b. Mar. 29, 1906

FRANCES JOSEPHINE   b. Nov. 29, 1909

JOHN WHITNEY   b. April 28, 1914
                       m. Oct.   1, 1938   Frances Jones
                       b. June 10, 1913

Issue of WEAVER McPHERSON & Edna M. Gore.
(H-76)

DOROTHY MAY   b. July   18, 1908
                               m. Oct. 28, 1928   Gale Buffington
                               b. Oct. 28, 1906

                  Issue;   DARLEEN
                           b. April 8, 1931
_____

DONALD   b. July   7,.1910
                               m. May 14, 1932   Roberta Mitchell
                               b. Aug. 15, 1910
                               (No issue)
_____

MARGARET   b. June   7, 1916
                               m. April 6, 1935   Noble Wright
                               b. Nov. 18, 1904

                  Issue;   DIANNE
                           b. July   31, 1937
_____

JOE   b. Oct.   2, 1921
_____

BEVERLEY (daughter)   b. Oct. 31, 1928
_____

Issue of IRVING RATTAN & Lottie L. Sherman.
(H-77)

ANGELO GROSVENOR   b. June 26, 1907
(1808 Octavia Street,   m. July   1936   Thelma
San Francisco, Cal.)   Richardson

                               b. May   2, 1911
_____

EMILY EDITH   b. April 24, 1910
(1137 Hyde Street,   m. May 26, 1935   Philip
San Francisco, Cal.)   Carlstroem

                  Issue;   PHILIP CHARLES
                           b. April 5, 1938
_____

ROBERT SHERMAN   b.   Aug. 7, 1916
_____

Issue of LLOYD EVAN & Valborg Hansen.
(H-77)

LLOYD EVAN, Jr.   b. May 12, 1929

_____

NORMAN SPROUL   b. Sept. 6, 1931

_____

ANITA MARGARET   b. May 8, 1936

_____

Issue of FORREST CUTTER & Mary Farrell.
(H-78)

FORREST HALBERT   b. July 28, 1904
                         m. Dec. 28, 1927   Adele Conwit

              Issue; FORREST RIDGWAY
                      b.

_____

JANET   b. Dec. 28, 1906

_____

MARY ELIZABETH   b. May 15, 1911
                         m.

_____

MARGARET ANN   b.   Oct. 1, 1912

_____

JOHN CLINTON   b.   June 8, 1914

_____

FRANCES ROSALIE   b. June 22, 1920

Issue of THOMAS WARE & Annie E. Evans.
(H-90)

SAMUEL EVANS
b. Oct. 17, 1857 d. Aug. 26, 1931
m. June 11, 1889 Martie MacQ. Bean
(of James M. & Rachel E. Borden)
b. April 21, 1871

Issue; THOMAS WARE   (Brooklyn, N. Y.)
b. April 6, 1890
m. June 11, 1919 Marguerite Schenck
(of Wm. P. & Elizabeth Ditmars)
b. June 28, 1895

ANNIE EVANS
b. Sept. 5, 1892
m. Oct. 21, 1914 Walter Bain Force
b. Aug. 18, 1882

Issue of EDWIN A. & Emma Wilson.
(H-90)

WALTER WILSON
b. Mar. 7, 1872 d. Jan. 27, 1932
(Un-married)

EDWIN
b.   d.   Dec., 1875
(infant)

JOSEPH G.
b. Dec. 3, 1876 d. Dec. 7, 1932
(Un-married)

INDEX

INDEX

INDEX

INDEX

INDEX

INDEX

INDEX

INDEX

INDEX

INDEX

INDEX

INDEX

INDEX

INDEX

INDEX

INDEX

INDEX

INDEX

INDEX

www.ingramcontent.com/pod-product-compliance
Lightning Source LLC
Chambersburg PA
CBHW031547260326
41914CB00002B/312